123
2 THOUGHTS AND A PRAYER

One Minute Inspirations

VOLUME – 1

BY
Dr. Viju Philip

He gives strength to the weary
and increases the power of the weak.

Even youths grow tired and weary,

and young men stumble and fall;

but those who hope in the Lord

will renew their strength.

They will soar on wings like eagles;

they will run and not grow weary,

they will walk and not be faint.

Isaiah 40:29-31

Table of Contents

INTRODUCTION

For most of us, life is busy, sometimes crazy, and of course, full of ups, downs, and turnarounds no matter what season we are in, because life is life. Life can also be in slow motion as you go through times of rest, healing, and being in the in-between of chaos. No matter what is happening to us or where we are in the scheme of things, it is important to find motivation because that is where our inspiration will come from. And where you find inspiration, you will also find motivation.

Having said that, I should also state there is only one thing that can truly motivate us no matter how we are or where we are, and that is the Word of God. God's Word gives us the right advice every time and guides us through our day.

Indeed, Jesus tells us the Holy Spirit has come to teach us and guide us. We are not left to our own way, but He will guide us to all truth.

Any day centered on the Word of God will be a blessed day. We still may face issues during the day, but daily studying the Word of God helps us to have an intimate relationship with God. When we know God and have an intimate relationship with Him, He brings application of the Word to the specific issues we face.

This book, **123, 2 Thoughts and A Prayer** (Volume 1), is a collection of one hundred twenty-three daily inspirations and prayers designed to inspire you to build an intimate relationship with God.

This book is not the Bible. However, each day will provide you with a Bible verse, a few thoughts to inspire your walk with the Lord, and a short prayer. Please do not limit your daily walk with the Lord to these few lines. Meditate on the Word of God and pray. Daily practicing these disciplines and growing closer to God will make you a strong person indeed. And that is our desire.

DAY ONE

SOW YOUR SEED

Sow your seed in the morning, and at evening let your hands not be idle, for you do not know which will succeed, whether this or that, or whether both will do equally well.
Ecclesiastes 11:6

Everything in life starts with a seed. Whatever we see manifested in the world and in our life today began as a seed. That is how God created the world. We know God is the ultimate Giver, and we reciprocate God's many blessings upon our lives by giving. Release your grip on earthly wealth. Then trust the Lord to meet your needs and share generously.

If you sow a godly thought, you will reap a godly act; when you sow a godly act, you will end up establishing a heavenly habit. Habits form the character, and eventually, that one godly thought will take you to your destiny!

PRAYER

Dear Father, my faith may be only the size of a tiny mustard seed, but I place that faith in You, my Lord, my Savior, my promise keeper, miracle worker. Just as every seed grows, I pray that my faith in you will grow and that I will act in faith. May I start trust you more than worrying over my needs. *IN JESUS' NAME WE ASK, AMEN!*

DAY TWO

ROOTING OUT FEAR

*The Lord is with me; I will not be afraid. What can mere
mortals do to me?*
Psalms 118:6

While you wrestle with fear-filled thoughts, you are consumed and robbed of the gift of living in the present moment. And it's in the present moment that God does His work in you.

Unfortunately, you are not where you should be. Fear super-imposes the future on the present. It empties today of its strength. Recognizing the spiritual battle of obsessive fear makes all the difference. It's the first step in understanding that you won't win the war on fear with your own strength.

As a believer, you have Christ. His grace allows you to overcome any situation, including the one that you are going through today!

PRAYER

Dear Father, fear threatens to overtake us, to hinder us from trusting You. We often seek to rely on ourselves, trusting in our own strength to accomplish our own desires. Lord, help us trust You and Your Word always. Help us be passionate about what matters and to care more about the eternal and less about the temporal.

Deliver us from the fear that holds us back so we might magnify the name of Jesus Christ, regardless of our work, our calling, and our involvements. FOR JESUS'S SAKE WE PRAY. AMEN.

DAY THREE

PLAN, BUT LET THE LORD LEAD

In his heart a man plans his course, but the LORD determines his steps.
Proverbs16:9

You tend to plan the course of your life and even your children's lives first, and then ask for God's blessing. But God's will for your life is to follow His lead at all times. The more you let God have His way, the more He can do in your life.

Do not get stuck where God has put a period. He did the best for you; believe that, and move on to the next chapter. Do not dwell on what you could not do. Because God will always work for the best of your life, not the second best!

PRAYER

Dear Father, send your Holy Spirit to teach, lead, and enlighten me. You said your Spirit would instruct me in everything and lead me to the truth. As I make decisions today, help me keep in mind what Jesus said.

Please grant me the tranquility that is beyond all comprehension when I feel overwhelmed by the choices I must make. To follow you with all my heart, soul, intellect, and might, I must clear my thoughts. IN THE NAME OF THE LORD JESUS CHRIST, AMEN.

DAY FOUR

GOD HOLDS YOU EVEN ON YOUR HARDEST DAYS

Even there, your hand will guide me, your right hand will hold me fast.
Psalms 139:10

God will bring some strange people on to your path just to prove to those who are trying to block your progress that it is not men, but GOD, HIMSELF, who is holding you. People will evaluate you based on your origin. However, they do not know your destination. God knows both!

Hold nothing tighter than you're holding God. He is holding you as you go through valleys and mountain tops.

PRAYER

Dear Father, my heart is filled with chaos and confusion. I feel as if I am drowning in my circumstances and my heart is filled with fear and confusion. I need Your strength to move on. I need Your strength to complete what is Your plan for me. I need the strength and peace only You can give. Right now, I choose to rest in You. IN JESUS'S NAME, I PRAY, AMEN.

DAY FIVE

HOPE IN DIFFICULT CIRCUMSTANCES

May the God of hope fill you with all joy and peace as you trust in him, so that you may overflow with hope by the power of the Holy Spirit.
Romans 15:13

When translated from Greek, the word hope means *'expectation of what is sure.'* This means that God was the God of what we can be assured of. He is not peddling false hope and shallow words of encouragement, but God can be trusted. He offers words of life when we are in despair.

We do not have to live discouraged. We do not have to be perpetually stuck in a place of despair or hopelessness. We can know hope through the power of the Holy Spirit. We do not have to make ourselves hopeful or conjure up joy where it does not exist. Hope is imparted through the power of the Holy Spirit.

PRAYER

Dear Father, let your hope and light shine upon me. Dear God, please help me be courageous when I am afraid, smart when I am clueless, comforted when I am alone, filled with hope when I feel rejected, and filled with peace when I am in turmoil. Please enable me to be strong when I am weak. Amen.

DAY SIX
SWEET SPICE

For we are to God the pleasing aroma of Christ among those who are being saved and those who are perishing. To the one we are an aroma that brings death; to the other, an aroma that brings life. And who is equal to such a task?
2 Corinthians 2:15-16

We carry the fragrance of Christ's character and love in our lives, whether we are conscious of it or not. People recognize the Lord in us as He permeates through our lives. In fact, the more we dwell in the Presence of the Lord, the more of His fragrance we exude to others.

Obedience to God's word is like a sweet spice. Like the hidden scent of honey locked up within the flowers, obedience gives off the fragrance of heaven. The perfume of Christ-likeness becomes evident to everyone.

PRAYER

Dear God, thank you for adopting me and transforming me from glory to glory through the power of the Holy Spirit. Dear God, create in me a pure heart and a generous spirit. In the name of Jesus, Amen.

DAY SEVEN

OUTLOOK DETERMINES THE OUTCOME!

Let us run with perseverance the race marked out for us,
fixing our eyes on Jesus, the pioneer and perfection of faith.
Hebrews 12:1b-2

Thoughts like 'things can never change for me' are more dangerous than the actual situation. We need to remind ourselves that God can change things.

How I look at a situation determines what comes to me! If we see only the problems, we will be defeated; but if we see the possibilities in the problems, we can have victory.

PRAYER

Dear God, thank you for allowing us to walk in the footsteps of Jesus Christ and for guiding us to the Cross. Father, help us let go of all that weighs us down and the sin that so easily entangles us. We want to be cheerful and full of faith, hope, and patience, since your kindness leads us forward. Help us keep our gaze fixed on You and only You, the creator and perfecter of our faith. In the name of Jesus, Amen.

DAY EIGHT

WHEN GOD SPEAKS IT IS ESTABLISHED

The Lord spoke to Moses in the tent of meeting in the Desert of Sinai on the first day of the second month of the second year after the Israelites came out of Egypt.
Numbers 1:1

If you are intimate with Christ, no man can ever intimidate you. Your closeness to Christ would enclose you in His favor.

Whenever God has spoken, regardless of to whom and it doesn't matter where, His words have become a divine principle which applies to anyone who trusts in Him. When God speaks, it is established.

PRAYER

Thank you, God, for establishing your words over my life. Help me be passionate about having a close connection with You. Speak life into me and establish your dominance over my problems. This I pray, in Jesus' name, Amen.

DAY NINE

SELF-RELIANCE?

*Can you drink the cup I drink or be baptized with the
baptism I am baptized with?*
Mark 10: 38

It's the pain and suffering that makes us finally realize that we are not in control of everything that happens in our lives and that we never were.

Just as the gym exposes deficiencies in your body's strength and stamina, the real-life situations that you go through expose your inner anxieties, your unrealistic regard for your talents, and your tendency to lie or shade the truth. In these instances, it will be far better to step back so that Jesus can move in!

PRAYER

Dear God, I must admit that I cannot serve you alone. My strength is insufficient. I depend on you and the power of the Holy Spirit to support me. Please give me courage and strength. In Jesus's name, I pray. Amen.

DAY TEN

PURPOSES EVOLVES FROM A PROCESS

Great are your purposes and mighty are your deeds...
Jeremiah 32:19a

The enemy opposes the purposes of God in your life. The good news is God, in his sovereignty, can make every scheme of the enemy to serve God's purposes.

What you go through is often the deep soul groaning for the purposes of God in and through you. It's a process. The key is to keep moving forward during this process until you realize the groaning has vanished. Chances are you will go through this process many times as you grow and change.

PRAYER

Dear God, thank you for letting me realize that everything I'm going through is for your glory. Help me grasp the process and strengthen me to keep moving forward without falling back. Send your Holy Spirit to soothe and guide me along this journey. Thank You, Father, in Heaven. In the name of Jesus, Amen.

DAY ELEVEN

TRUST AND PRAYER

I know that you can do all things; no purpose of yours can be thwarted.
Job 42:2

Human plans will always fail, often because the planner has overlooked some detail. Something unforeseen arises and suddenly plans collapse. However, God's plan is all-inclusive. Every contingency is considered in God's plan. God's plan includes seemingly insignificant details. That's why some things are delayed, because God is currently working on those details.

Trusting God and praying to Him causes all situations to align with the purposes of God. Trust and prayer combine our weakness with God's omnipotent forces.

PRAYER

Dear God, thank you for being God, the source of all power in heaven and on earth. When I look at the heavens and the extraordinary works You have created, I know nothing is impossible for You. Help me live in humble surrender to the prompting of Your Spirit. I believe You can do anything, and nothing you plan is impossible. Thank You, in the name of Jesus, AMEN.

DAY TWELVE

ENDURE, ALL WILL BE FOR GOOD

The LORD works out everything to its proper end...
Proverbs 16:4

All it takes from God is just a shift. With that one shift in your life, the very trajectory of your life will change and change the lives of your descendants.

The things that you went through brought you where you are today! If it weren't for those isolations and pain, you wouldn't have the power of God. God is making you the solution to someone's problem. Every gift you have will make bigger room for you to bring glory to God's name! You will see why you had to endure what you went through!

PRAYER

Dear God, thank You for the numerous truths concealed inside the lovely pages of Your Word. From now on, surround me with insight and give me the spirit to do everything for Your glory. I ask that the words I speak and the plans I make for my life are precisely aligned with Your Word and Your desire. I entrust my works to you, Lord, and beg that you arrange my thoughts, so I do not waver. Amen.

DAY THIRTEEN

KEEP GOING PASSIONATELY

I will instruct you and teach you in the way you should go; I will counsel you with my eye upon you.
Psalms 32:8

God pledges to keep a close eye on us while He continues to teach and guide us in the redemption route. He will not abandon us because He knows that without His guidance and watchful eye on us, we will wander from the road of righteousness like sheep.

The Lord will teach you in the way you should go, the path to finding your purpose on earth, so you can fulfill your reason for existence. Are you passionate about something? Keep working toward it. That's the route to finding your purpose! Your passion will bring you the courage to fulfill your vision. So, vision and passion are all related to your purpose.

PRAYER

Dear God, thank you for your promise to watch over me while I enjoy your limitless guidance and counseling. With this, I am assured that I am not alone. Thank you, heavenly Father. Help me, Oh Lord, to recognize your instructions and follow you with the spirit of obedience. Help me discover my purpose on earth, so I can live a fulfilled life. This I pray, in Jesus's name, Amen.

DAY FOURTEEN

TAKE FAITH STEPS

*... if you have faith as small as a mustard seed,
you can say to this mountain, 'Move from here to there,'
and it will move...*
Matthew 17:20

You do not need to know all the small details to take your faith step. You need to be content with the 'seed' detail, the little detail you have. That is the content for the 'mustard seed faith.'

All you need is a self-emptied, dependent assurance in God's character and promises to take your faith steps. All the strength and power come from the object of faith, God himself.

PRAYER

Dear God, help me in my desire to serve you while remaining confident in your supply of power, courage, and instruction. I ask you to strengthen my faith when I say little prayers. Help me see more of You in the simplest things so my faith in Your goodness can grow. *I believe you have answered. Amen.*

DAY FIFTEEN

STAY CONNECTED TO THE SHEPHERD

The Lord is my shepherd; I shall not want.
Psalms 23:1

A shepherd is a close and intimate relationship. Whereas a king might do what's best for most of his people, a shepherd knows each one of his sheep.

"The Lord is my shepherd; I shall not want" is a reminder of the fact that there is no satisfaction outside of God. Every void and every need in your life is fulfilled by God himself.

PRAYER

Dear God, Thank You for being my wonderful Shepherd. Thank you for your leadership and sovereignty. Thank you for your wisdom and concern throughout our lives. I adore you because you are all I need; you are our refuge and hope. In Jesus's name, AMEN.

DAY SIXTEEN

THROUGH THE VALLEY

Even though I walk through the valley of the
shadow of death,
Psalms 23:4

The Shepherd is not taking you 'to' the valley. He is taking you 'through' the valley. In other words, you are going to make it.

Even when you may have several reasons to be afraid, you do not need to be fearful because of who is with you. The Shepherd will take care of you. He knows what He is doing and has your best interests in mind.

PRAYER

Dear God, thank You for the assurance that I don't have to face death alone. Thank you for giving me the fortitude to keep going, even in the darkest of circumstances. I shall be brave and fearless, knowing that You are always with me, even when it is tough for me to see. I seek your direction and listen for your voice to take me over death's gloomy valley and into your holy and beautiful presence in victory and joy. This I pray boldly in Jesus's name. Amen.

DAY SEVENTEEN

DO NOT GIVE THE ENEMY A SEAT AT YOUR TABLE

You prepare a table before me in the presence of my enemies.
Psalms 23:5

The table is in the presence of the enemies because God wants you to know that you'll always have enough for every moment, every struggle. He'll sustain you every dark night. And God wants the enemies to watch you shine.

Do not give in to sin or despair. Take every thought captive. Bind every thought in Jesus' name that doesn't come from God. Fill your mind with the goodness and richness of Scripture. Or simply said, do not give the enemy a seat at your table.

PRAYER

Dear God, thank you for making my enemies watch me shine. Thank you for standing right there with me, uplifting me right in front of my enemies. Today, I pray You sustain me in every dark night. I pray you purify my thoughts and help me not give in to sin or despair and that you fill my mouth and mind with the goodness and richness of your words. This I ask Father, in Jesus's name, Amen.

DAY EIGHTEEN

PROBLEMS CAN BECOME A GIFT

Remember the Lord, who is great and awesome...
Nehemiah4:14

You cannot run away from problems. They will come, and offenses will come. See that you do not cause offense. See that you live on a higher tide. See that your tongue and your heart are aligned properly.

Problems can become a gift if we seize them as an opportunity to strengthen our faith in the Lord Jesus. They can make us better people.

PRAYER

Dear God, I know You are great and awesome. I know You are greater than my problems and my enemies, which in return gives me the assurance that my battle has been won. Thank You, Lord. Today I pray You reveal every enemy's plan over my life, so I can stand in prayer to You, the great God, against the enemy. So that I can live for God as a witness to everyone around me. Amen.

DAY NINETEEN

CHRIST'S AMBASSADORS

We are therefore Christ's ambassadors, as though God were making his appeal through us.
2 Corinthians 5:20

Ambassadors represent something much bigger than they themselves are. They have always been symbolic incarnations of the sovereignty of their nations and the dignity of their leader.

Knowledge and wisdom are packaged in a person. If that person does not embody the virtues of the kingdom he serves, he will undermine his message and handicap his mission.

PRAYER

Dear God, thank You for Your wonderful goodness, loving mercy, and patience with me and all humanity. Help me be a worthy witness to the truth of Your Word and to fearlessly proclaim the message of reconciliation to everyone I come into contact with. Amen, in Jesus's name.

DAY TWENTY

KNOWLEDGE AND KNOWINGNESS

Come unto me, all you who are weary and burdened, and I will give you rest.
Matthew11:28

There is knowledge, and then there is knowingness. You can read in the Bible that you are supposed to always trust God. It is possible that you understand this fully and acknowledge in your head that you need to trust God. But still, you grow weary and burdened because the knowledge never became real.

The load becomes overbearing when we try to take over and do the pulling or pushing in your own strength. Do not let your burdens make you lose your joy in Christ. Submit to the Lordship of Jesus Christ.

PRAYER

Dear God, thank You for assisting me and leading me through my days. I am glad for the blessing of being able to speak with You now that the hurdle of sin has been erased. Thank You for promising to give me genuine peace in my spirit and perfect contentment in my heart. I have a lot on my mind and many obligations right now. I beg you to grant me rest for my exhausted body and mind. Please relieve me of my responsibilities, console me, and give my soul rest so I can be joyous in your name. Amen.

DAY TWENTY-ONE
JOYFUL SPIRIT

Consider it pure joy, my brothers and sisters, whenever you face trials of many kinds.
James 1:2

Christian joy includes a profoundly deep sense of peace and comfort that sustains believers even during sickness, persecution, and various suffering. The reason for this joy resides in the life, death, and resurrection of Jesus Christ.

A joyful spirit is not one that is happy all the time, no matter the circumstances. Rather, it has a firm foundation of peace and understanding that no matter what happens, God loves us, knows us, and will never leave us. This truly is the highest blessing.

PRAYER

Dear God, you offer us ultimate blessedness in your presence always, and for that, we humbly thank you. May our spirit reflect the joy of the hope we have in you. In Christ we pray. Amen.

DAY TWENTY-TWO
DELIVERED OUT

For He has rescued us from the dominion of darkness and
brought us into the kingdom of the Son He loves.
Colossians1:13

Springtime brings longer days and shorter nights. So, when the season changes from winter into spring and summer, darkness is reduced, and more light is seen. The point here is that you are not only delivered out of something but are also brought into something as well. This is how your spiritual condition is. Both do not go together. In Jesus, there is enough light for those who want to trust Him and enough darkness to blind those who don't.

PRAYER

Dear God, thank You, Almighty Father, for rescuing me from the evil dominion and repositioning me to the kingdom of Your dear Son. Neither my words nor my actions will ever be able to repay the gift you have given me in Jesus. I appreciate you and give my life as a sacrifice of praise for everything You have done, all that you have given me, and all that this has cost you. Jesus, may your holy name be blessed. Amen.

DAY TWENTY-THREE
STAY BLESSED

My foes have trampled upon me all day long, for they are many who fight proudly against me.
Psalms 56:2

The enemy attacks those the most, who carry things that are valuable most for the Kingdom.

Every blessing is a point of attack. However, your faith in God, humility, and obedience to God's word will position you for the next level of blessings.

PRAYER

Dear God, I thank You for being my God, and I trust You to see me through the hardships and temptations I am experiencing today. You know my enemies, and you know how many there are. Help me overcome them, Lord. Father, please grant me the grace to trust You more. Amen.

DAY TWENTY-FOUR

NO WEAPON WILL PROSPER AGAINST YOU

What if the LORD had not been on our side when people attacked us?
Psalms124:2

The protection of God toward His children has not diminished over the past 2000-plus years. He still sits on His great throne, and His train still fills the temple.

The Lord who calmed storms, raised dead men to life, and multiplied fishes and loaves to feed thousands is the same God you have today. No weapon will ever prosper against you!

PRAYER

Dear God, thank You for Your unshaken protection. Thank you for remaining firm in watching over my soul and rescuing me from every evil hurdle. Thank you for the assurance of safety. Now I can rest knowing no weapon fashioned against me shall prosper. Blessed be your holy name, Jesus. Amen.

DAY TWENTY-FIVE

CHECK WHAT YOU ARE STORING

*Put on the full armor of God, so that you will be able to
stand firm against the schemes of the devil.*
Ephesians 6:11

The armor-bearer of sin is confidence in oneself. Such confidence exposes the heart to many dangers. Those who put on the full armor of God will combat the temptations of the world, the flesh, and the devil.

The person trusting in the armor of God is fully armed at all points. God has made us invulnerable to outside attacks. The only vulnerable place in your armor is where you leave it exposed. What you store inside your heart can lead you to destruction. Put on the full armor of God and continuously check what you are storing inside your heart.

PRAYER

Dear God, I am grateful that You chose to regard me as Your son. I know you'll never abandon me. I also believe you can defeat the enemy. I beg that you empower me in the areas where I am most prone to sin or laziness. Please assist me in fastening Your belt of truth around my waist. Fill me with the Bible's knowledge. Rekindle my desire to pursue your purity with zeal. I hope You will keep me from being misled by worldly deception and wicked lies. Amen.

DAY TWENTY-SIX

KINDNESS CAN MELT YOUR WORLD

Be kind to one another, tenderhearted, forgiving one another, as God in Christ forgave you
Ephesians 4:32

Mother Teresa said, "Let there be kindness in our face, in your eyes, in your smile, in the warmth of your greeting... Don't only give your care, but give your heart as well."

Kindness makes a person attractive. If you want to win your world, melt it, do not hammer it.

PRAYER

Dear God, thank You for forgiving me through grace through trust in Christ. Please forgive me for whatever grudges I've had against You or others. Please assist me in showing compassion to others. When something is unclear, please help me by clarifying it. To the glory of Christ, enable me to live my life as unto Him, to be slow to anger, quick to forgive, and overflowing with steadfast love, compassion, sympathy, tolerance, and kindness. Amen.

DAY TWENTY-SEVEN
GOD'S FAVOR ZONE

You bless the righteous, O Lord; you cover him with favor as with a shield.
Psalm 5:12

God's favor will not allow you to break down but will accelerate you toward a breakthrough.

The moment you decide to 'walk in a right relationship' with God, you are entering a 'favor-zone.' God is always pleased to send extraordinary favors to those who walk according to Kingdom principles.

PRAYER

Dear God, thank You for Your divine mercy, which I experience daily in my activities. Thank You for shielding me with Your favor and blessing the virtuous, in which I share. I pray You will help me work well with you. Please help me labor in accordance with the Kingdom values. This I ask. Amen.

DAY TWENTY-EIGHT
CHILD OF GOD

See what kind of love the Father has given to us, that we should be called children of God; and so we are.
1 John 3:1

A child of God can trust God's directives will always be right and best. Since the privilege of being a child of God stems from the Father's unconditional love, the best response is whole-hearted obedience.

To call yourself a child of God is one thing. To be called a child of God by those around us is another thing. The latter brings more glory to God.

PRAYER

Dear God, thank you for the tremendous blessing of being Your child. Thank You for loving me enough to save me and calling me Your child through Christ. Father, I eagerly await what I can learn now about what being Your child means, and I eagerly await the day when I will meet You face-to-face and truly comprehend the significance of this delight.

DAY TWENTY-NINE
THE GOD – DIRECTED LIFE

*Many are the afflictions of the righteous, but the LORD
delivers him out of them all.*
Psalms 34:19

The journey for a child of God can be tough and rough. But the arrival is worth it.

A righteous person is a 'God-directed' person who knows the afflictions in life will not derail his journey but put him back on the right track.

PRAYER

Dear God, thank you for your beautiful promises. Provide me with the faith I need to know that whatever occurs in my life will not separate me from your love and salvation for me. Help me and deliver me in accordance with Your promise and make my life a witness to Your faithfulness. In Jesus's name, I pray. Amen.

DAY THIRTY
TRUST GOD STRONGLY

When I am afraid, I put my trust in you.
Psalms 56:3

When in a storm, visibility becomes poor. That's why God said to put your trust in Him. Walk by faith when visibility ahead is difficult.

Do not be afraid of anything and pray about everything. Trust God strongly, trust His word, and trust the process. You will have no surprises.

PRAYER

Dear God, thank You for Your grace that allows me to have absolute faith in you. Father, help me remain solid in my confidence in you and please help me cast off every spirit of fear so I can confidently trust the process and your words. Amen.

DAY THIRTY-ONE
TRUST IS A PROCESS

Who has known the mind of the Lord?
Or who has been his counselor?
Romans11:36

You can never know what God is doing. Sometimes He might be cleaning you up. Don't go digging back through the trash. Allow Him to do what He wants to do.

Trust is a process that begins with God working in you and you moving out of the way for Him to do the things your mind can never comprehend.

PRAYER

Dear God, thank you for your amazing generosity. Lord, direct our steps and open our hearts to your Word. Teach me to be filled with love and abounding with faith while trusting the process. In Jesus's name, Amen.

DAY THIRTY-TWO
GOD, THE FATHER

A father to the fatherless, a defender of widows,
is God in his holy dwelling.
God sets the lonely in families,
he leads out the prisoners with singing;
but the rebellious live in a sun-scorched land.
Psalm 68:5-6

"Father" is God's self-revealed designation. Since God is your Father, the implications are staggering. It means you can talk to Him and relate to Him on a personal and intimate basis. Most importantly, you have someone who will always defend you.

God occupies all the difficult situations humanity has endured, being fatherless, being a widow, being a prisoner or any other circumstances, you may be facing. And so, He is your father.

PRAYER

Dear God, I am thankful that I may rely on You in times of hardship, illness, or loneliness; I know in my heart, Lord, that I am not alone since You are with me. I feel unwell, terrified, and alone. Please, Lord, make me healthy again soon and lift my drooping spirit. You have the power to cure me and remove my deepest wounds. I pray You will use Your Word and Your people to alleviate some of my suffering. This I pray, Amen.

DAY THIRTY-THREE

A SECURE FORTRESS

Whoever fears the Lord has a secure fortress,
and for their children it will be a refuge.
Proverbs14:26

The more deeply you fear the Lord, the more fortified you will be against every onslaught against your lives and against your children.

Fear of the Lord is the very attitude to never leave His presence, His love, His care, and His protection.

PRAYER

Dear God, thank you for the assurance you provide every time I follow your Word. I'm prepared to obey You, to be someone who fears You and avoids evil, so that my heart doesn't leave You and so I may magnify You and accept Your guidance in everything. Teach me to have a healthy respect of you and the life you've chosen for me. Amen.

DAY THIRTY-FOUR

GOD'S PLAN FOR YOU IS BIGGER

Jesus looked at them and said, "With man this is impossible, but with God all things are possible.."
Matthew 19:26

God will never give you a dream that matches your training, background, upbringing or even what you have. The dream God gives you will need faith in Him and nothing else.

God's plan for you is bigger than what you have for yourself. Do not look at yourself based on what you are but look at yourself based on who your creator is.

PRAYER

Dear God, thank You for equipping me with Your Spirit to do all to which I am called. Thank You for making what I thought was impossible possible for You. Please help me put my reliance on You rather than on my talents and abilities. In Jesus's name, I declare I can accomplish anything! Amen.

DAY THIRTY-FIVE

REVELATION IS LINKED TO OBEDIENCE

... I have now seen the One who sees me.
Genesis 16:13

Even when you cannot see yourself or your next step, God sees your value. He sees you the way you are even when you try to hide yourself, your emotions, your fear, and your tears. God will craft a beautiful you out of all your mess.

You will know about God only to the extent of your obedience. Revelation is linked to obedience.

PRAYER

Dear God, it is good to know You see me. You see and know, even when I believe no one sees or knows about my difficulties. I ask for grace amid loneliness, hurt, sorrow, obstacles, and tribulations and to know you are present. I pray I won't forget that Your gaze is always on me. In the name of Jesus, Amen.

DAY THIRTY-SIX
DO NOT BE INTIMIDATED

A thousand may fall at your side, ten thousand at your right hand, but it will not come near you.
Psalm 91:7

A sincere worship will strengthen you and will give you a sense of God's presence, provision, protection and power. Worship will change how you look at the circumstances.

Identify all the giants in your life. Identify and slay them. Do not be intimidated by failures and setbacks. A man who is intimate with God will not be intimidated by anyone or anything else.

PRAYER

Dear God, thank You for Your tremendous protection over my family and myself. Lord, it's frequently difficult to hear of so many people getting sick and dying, which may naturally bring dread and anxiety. Help us take those frightening thoughts captive. Lord, help us rely on You. Help us have more confidence in You, in the name of Jesus. Amen.

DAY THIRTY-SEVEN
POWER OF REDEMPTION

Do not fear, for I have redeemed you;
I have summoned you by name; you are mine...
Isaiah43:1

Since Jesus is your redeemer, you don't have to live in regret. Only Jesus can be trusted for perfect redemption.

The boldness of a child of God is seen through their wounds and deep scars. When people see them, they appreciate the power of redemption more than ever.

PRAYER

Dear God, thank You for Your generous promises to Israel and to Your new creation in Christ. Thank you for upholding your promises. Thank You for redeeming me, calling me by name, and making me Yours by grace through faith. Please shower your people with awe-inspiring reminders of your steadfast presence and use us to bring you glory. AMEN.

DAY THIRTY-EIGHT

THE LORD YOUR GOD GOES WITH YOU

Be strong and courageous. Do not be afraid or terrified because of them, for the Lord your God goes with you; he will never leave you nor forsake you.
Deuteronomy31:6

When you look at what is ahead of you, it might look like a big thing. If you believe in a God who controls the universe, then you should believe that God can also handle your big and small things.

Continuous effort—keeping on, moving on—is the key to feeling the Lord God moving ahead of you. You can never be strengthened if you are at a standstill.

PRAYER

Dear God, thank you for always being there to help me through life's challenges. I know you're in control. I pray you open my thoughts so that I can be more aware of your presence. Please help me rely on, trust in, and confide in you. I beg you to give me strength and help me eliminate my anxiety. I know you will not abandon me. Amen.

DAY THIRTY-NINE

PROMISES OF GOD ARE 'YES'

For no matter how many promises God has made, they are
"Yes" in Christ.
2 Corinthians 1:20

Sometimes, the smallest step taken in the right direction at the right moment leads you to the biggest achievement in life.

Adore the riches in every promise of God. They will lead you from glory to glory.

PRAYER

Dear God, thank you for being faithful to me! Thank You for Your Word, which is a lamp to my feet, a light to my way, and a witness to Your tremendous love for me. I beg Please give as you will to every hope and hunger in my heart. In the name of Jesus, Amen.

DAY FORTY

BEARING FRUITS

... Neither can you bear fruit unless you remain in me.
John 15:4

Not all seeds bear good fruit. Most seeds bear fruit in due season. The seed planted beside the water can grow into a tree. The more the tree is shaken by the wind, the deeper it will strike its roots into the ground.

The union between remaining in Christ and bearing fruit is significant. The effects of this union can change lives and generations.

PRAYER

Dear God, today, I pray to abide in You, rest in Your love, and believe Your Word. I want to think properly, behave intelligently, and communicate with kindness. I aim to have my behaviors reflect your magnificence. I beg you to abide with me, console me, strengthen me, and fill me with knowledge. This I pray in Jesus's name, Amen.

DAY FORTY-ONE

BE INSTRUCTED BY GOD

I will instruct you and teach you in the way you should go;
I will counsel you with my loving eye on you.
Psalms 32:8

Following God's instructions leads to a blessed life because His instructions come with training and encouragement.

Whose instruction you follow determines the future you create. The uncertainty you experience is your soul crying for instructions. If you had been instructed, then uncertainty would not have happened.

PRAYER

Dear God, Thank You for allowing me to confess my flaws to You and for Your faithfulness and justice in forgiving all my sins and cleansing me from all unrighteousness. I've been going in the wrong direction. I'm at a crossroads and don't know what to do. I've failed to listen to Your voice many times, gone my own way, and fell flat on my face! Please help me. Bring me back on track, guide me away from ruin. Help me develop in grace, faith, and drawing ever closer to You. This I pray in the name of Jesus, Amen.

DAY FORTY-TWO
THE ALL-KNOWING GOD

Great is our Lord and mighty in power;
his understanding has no limit.
Psalms 147:5

You can manage life with very little, but you can never manage life without God. You cannot live for God by appointment, giving him certain times and keeping Him out of your life at other times. He is what you need first, foremost, and always. He is the only one who you can't do without!

God is All-Knowing. He knows perfectly what He is doing. When you cannot understand His ways, trust His heart. Everything will work out much better than you can imagine.

PRAYER

Dear God, thank You for promising to mend my brokenness and heal my pain. I know You are willing and capable of carrying me through whatever predicament life may throw at me. As I pray for a humble heart, aid me in my daily walk, and help me totally surrender to you. Amen.

DAY FORTY-THREE
THE WORKS OF THE WORD

All Scripture is God-breathed and is useful for teaching, rebuking, correcting and training in righteousness, so that the servant of God may be thoroughly equipped for every good work.
2 Timothy 3:16-17

The Holy Bible is not a textbook, and we cannot compare it with the Koran, the Buddhist scriptures, the Book of Mormon, and the like. The Bible can't be compared with these books because it is undoubtedly God's breath, God's wind, and God's words written to educate, correct, rebuke, and destroy the works of Satan while also training its readers in righteousness.

All Scripture is breathed out by God.. This explains that the Bible possesses power and is useful for God's people. It is "the word of God [that is] living and active, sharper than any two-edged sword, piercing to the division of soul and spirit, of joints and marrow, and discerning the thoughts and intentions of the heart." The Scriptures are the most valuable thing we have as Christians, and we are compelled to value them, pursue them, and study them. Because the more we do, the more we grow in Christ and become armed with spiritual weapons to subdue the world.

PRAYER

Thank You, kind Father, for the inspired Scriptures. Thank you for Your daily counsel. Teach, shape, and empower me with the words I need to put the Bible into action. Convict, instruct, and train me by the active, strong divine Word of truth, so I may be prepared to carry out the task You have assigned to me. Use me as a wisdom tool for teaching your Word to expand your kingdom. In your holy name, amen.

DAY FORTY-FOUR

CAST ALL YOUR BURDENS UPON THE LORD

Cast all your anxiety on him because he cares for you.
1 Peter 5:7

Are you weary of dealing with the same old issues over and over? Is it bothering you to the point that it's weighing you down? The book of Proverbs 12:25a says, "Anxiety in a man's heart weighs him down." It's time to quit attempting to control what's out of your control and surrender everything to God.

The more anxieties you pile on yourself, the more anxious your thoughts, emotions, and physical body become. Put your burdens on him and let him bear your problems. Stop putting your desire for control over His love. Remember, He said, "Come to me, all you who are weary and burdened, and I will give you rest. He is a compassionate God who longs to give you rest. He promised to walk alongside us and ease our burdens. He knows it all. Allow Him to fill you with His peace through His plans.

PRAYER

Loving Father and Almighty God, I come to You today casting my anxieties, frustration, and cares on You. I will do my best not to dwell on them and trust that you will do what is best for me. I choose to believe in Your Word and have faith that You are working behind the scenes on my behalf and that none of these are too big for you to handle. I trust you, Oh God. You are the God of the universe. Thank you, and blessed be your holy name. Amen.

DAY FORTY-FIVE

ALL SPIRITUAL BLESSINGS...

Praise be to the God and Father of our Lord Jesus Christ,
who has blessed us in the heavenly realms with every
spiritual blessing in Christ.
Ephesians 1:3

Being blessed isn't just about the earthly blessings. Because whenever the word I am blessed is being talked about, we tend to accept that it's about the blessings of health, family, happiness, reputation, food, comfort, love, and the likes. Well, these are not bad to have; truth be told, they are man's necessities, real blessings for which a man should be grateful. However, these blessings are not what the Apostle Paul was talking about. What kind of blessings is he talking about? The spiritual blessings that God has blessed us with are truly 'out of this world.' They give us a wonderful foretaste of heaven so that we will choose to set our affection on things above rather than on things on the earth.

The first 'blessing' is actually not about our own personal fulfillment at all. Rather, he is talking here about "spiritual blessings in the heavenly places." These are blessings that have to do with God's Holy Spirit and the spiritual dimension of life. We don't often dwell on the spiritual dimension of life because it's not right in our faces, and sometimes it seems so distant and unreal. But in fact, it's these spiritual blessings that really matter. These blessings are secure, as it includes being chosen, forgiven, adopted, and given knowledge and hope.

PRAYER

Thank you, God. I come before thee with hymns of praise in my heart for all the spiritual gifts You have bestowed on me for trusting in your son, Lord Jesus, for redemption. Thank You for redeeming my soul and bestowing your spirit on me, Who has put me in Christ and seated me with Him in heavenly realms. May my desires be in accordance with Your plan for my life so that I may enjoy all the spiritual blessings that are mine through Christ Jesus. Amen.

DAY FORTY-SIX
THE GIFT OF GRACE

... how much more will those who receive God's abundant provision of grace and of the gift of righteousness reign in life through the one man, Jesus Christ!
Romans 5:17

In the beginning, humans sinned which separated us from God, paving the path for sin to reign and ultimately bring death. But, in His boundless mercy, God sent His son (Christ) to suffer for our sins to provide God's free gift of grace to those who believe. For it is in Jesus' grace that we live. Grace reigns by guiding people to eternal life via God's covenant of righteousness in the life of our Lord Jesus (reconciliation to God). And now that sin has been shattered by the power of grace, we can now boast that we have grace bigger than all our sins.

Romans chapter five clearly outlines the benefits of being pronounced righteous by God as a result of our unwavering trust in Christ Jesus. And we are now richly endowed with abundance and peace with God while keeping steadfast in His grace.

PRAYER

Thank you, God. I come to you with a grateful heart for the abundance of grace you have bestowed upon me. You have done so much to bring mankind's lost and fallen race back into Your fold. I am glad for the gift of righteousness and the wonderful promises that all Your children shall reign in life through Jesus Christ, Who identified with my sin and paid the full penalty that I deserve so that I can share in Your eternal life. I will no longer dwell on the knowledge that I am a sinner. Father, I bless You because there is still a place in Christ for me to rule.

DAY FORTY-SEVEN
A REASON FOR HOPE

... since we are receiving a kingdom that cannot be shaken,
let us be thankful,
Hebrews 12:28

This Bible passage tells us that our stability, joy, and hope are founded on a reality larger than this current world with all of its empires and promises! Our identity and future depend not on what this fleeting world offers. It is not reliant on the possibility of events occurring right now. Our hope is a happy hope of being members of a Kingdom that will never fail and of a King who will rule gloriously forever, and that we will be members of that unshaken Kingdom forever! A joyful expectation of a stable future!

The acknowledgment of God's immense mercy and grace for sinners like us should urge us to give our bodies as a pure and acceptable living sacrifice to God. "Let us be thankful;" this alone should inspire us to glorify God even in the middle of a terrible reality on this earth! All the Lord has done for us should motivate us to be genuine and have eternal worship, heartfelt praise, and sincere devotion.

PRAYER

Dear God, thank you for giving me a fresh cause to hope and for ensuring a position in your matchless, unbreakable, and unconquerable Kingdom. Thank You for the assurance of me being rescued by grace through trust in Christ. Remind us of what we have in You today so that we might worship You with reverence, amazement, and confidence. Please assist us in worshipping well and fulfilling what You want of us. In Jesus's name, we pray, amen!

DAY FORTY-EIGHT
OUT OF THE MOUTH

What goes into someone's mouth does not defile them, but what comes out of their mouth, that is what defiles them.
Matthew 15:11

We currently live in a topsy-turvy world where people are more concerned with what they consume than what they say. A society in which millions of individuals are unconcerned about the consequences of their actions. However, this Bible verse clearly illustrates that defilement is not an external phenomenon.

What is in the heart is what "defiles" it. What "defiles" the heart is what is in it. Our deeds are assessed in light of what God discovers in our souls. The evil connected with external action is defined by the motivation of the person undertaking it. Acts that are "good" are not "good" if they are motivated by legalism or performed for the wrong motives.

As we reflect on Jesus's teachings, let us strive to live as unto the Lord, never forgetting that what comes out of the mouth defiles the man or woman, not what goes into it. Our words are an astonishingly accurate assessment of our hearts and lives. The Bible says in Matthew 12:34 that "out of the abundance of the heart, the mouth speaks!" And our hearts should point others to truth. "Therefore, allow your light to shine so brightly before men that they may see your good works and praise your Father in heaven." (Matthew 5:16)

PRAYER

Dear God, I want you to redeem my heart, search me, and uproot any insincerity and blemish You find there. Help me today, Lord, to avoid anything that can corrupt and taint my heart toward You and Your children. Let the words of my mouth be a reflection of a heart that respects you in thought, expression, and deed. I ask for the power of the Spirit to help me with this commitment. In Jesus's name, I pray, AMEN.

DAY FORTY-NINE
GOD IS SUFFICIENT

*And my God will meet all your needs according to the riches
of his glory in Christ Jesus.*
Philippians 4:19

God is sufficient, and He will never leave those who seek Him. He will meet our physical, physiological, and spiritual needs. One exciting interpretation of this chapter is that it is connected to God's desire to reward us for our achievements. When we are generous with our resources, abilities, and time for God's kingdom, God delights in being even more gracious to us than we are to Him. He is overflowing with gracious mercy and bubbling over with loving-kindness. He does not make failing promises. He is loyal to His words, and His fullness of compassion covers everything and anything that we may need.

Paul wrote this Bible passage to the Philippians, thanking them for generously providing for his needs while in prison. He expressed his gratefulness in the Bible passage and, at the same time, reminds us to be content in any circumstances, whether we have minimal necessities or abundance, since we can rely on God who will never fail us.

PRAYER

Dear God, I come before you to worship Your holy name and submit my needs to You, knowing that You care about my necessities now and the eternal wealth that You have prepared for me in heaven. I now have a deep conviction in Your provision, and I know You are adequate even in terrible times. Help me have peace of mind knowing that my salvation is safe and that material things are not my priority. In Jesus's name, I pray, AMEN.

DAY FIFTY

GOD IS NOT FINISHED YET

... being confident of this, that he who began a good work in you will carry it on to completion until the day of Christ Jesus.
Philippians 1:6

God is not finished; He is not a God who abandons His works. Knowing this helps bring tremendous comfort and happiness to all believers. Because, if we look at the state of the world, the state of the church, and even the state of our own lives, we know that if this were the end of the narrative, we would all be in severe danger. However, this is not the end. God is still active. He's not finished yet. Paul wrote to the Philippian church to encourage them as gospel partners and to help them in their Christian lives.

You should thus stop worrying as a believer because "He will totally and completely finish what He has begun." That implies He will preserve us in faith and never abandon us from now until the end of our life, no matter what happens or the circumstances that emerge. He is not through yet! The same God who began a good work in you will see it finished.

PRAYER

Dear God, thank You for the incredible work you've begun in me; I can see your fingerprints and grace guiding me to where I am now. Dear Lord, in Your love and mercy, please finish and perfect the good work You have begun for my everlasting benefit. AMEN, in Jesus's name.

DAY FIFTY-ONE

OVERCOMING TEMPTATION

Submit yourselves, then, to God. Resist the devil, and he will flee from you.
James 4:7

Every single person on the planet is either a follower of God or a not a follower of God. There is no middle ground. However, this verse instructs us to "submit ourselves to God." That is, we should pledge our loyalty to God! But, to rekindle that relationship with God, discover grace, and reestablish our friendship, we must first submit to His counsel. We must abandon the notion that we may live our lives however we like. We must surrender the control of our lives to God. Even though sometimes His instructions make us uncomfortable, we must obey them. By listening to God's counsel, you can avoid the dirt and immorality of the world. We must "fight Satan" and obey God.

To be submissive to God, we must oppose the devil at all costs. Most of the time, we allow our desires and passions to flare up within us, making it seem complicated to do anything but commit sin to quell those feelings. However, here is a reassuring word from God, "Battle the devil and it shall flee." You can battle the devil, and he will flee. This is not a lost cause. You can fight against drunkenness and alcoholism. You can combat sexual immorality and desire. You can get over your pride. You can deal with anger and hate. You are capable of fighting your tongue. You can triumph against selfishness. Never, ever quit. Confront the demon. If you fight him, you will see him flee.

PRAYER

Dear God, thank you for the strength you give me every day and the knowledge that I have power over the devil. I beg you to assist me in resisting the devil and any of his agents. Help me overcome any temptations that come my way. Assist me in doing what is best rather than what is most comfortable. Please assist me in remaining focused on Christ's paths. In Jesus's Name, Amen.

DAY FIFTY-TWO

OVERCOMING TEMPTATION

"You of little faith," he said, "why did you doubt?"
Matthew 14:31

Sometimes the flesh in us makes us want to doubt God. While it leaves us drowning in fear of the unknown, God remains unchanged, the same as His promises, which include, "When you pass through the waters, I will be with You." This alone should always motivate you in tough times. Fear may cause you to lose sight of God's beautiful promises and make your faith waver but never let fear win. Fix your gaze on Jesus in every problematic, dangerous, or painful situation in life, for fear and faith are incompatible collaborators.

Cling to and treasure your "little faith." Jesus is with us, and we belong to Him. He tells us this repeatedly, yet we never seem to get it. We obsess about little issues and wonder why our faith wavers. He is aware of our limitations and imperfections, short-comings and inadequacies, and fears and anxieties, yet He loves us. He instructs you to lift your eyes and look at Him, and he promises everything will be fine. He'll keep you safe from the storm. When the storms threaten to sweep you away, remember that you have a God capable of rescuing you from what looks to be an ocean of problems, sadness, annoyance, or panic.

PRAYER

Dear God, thank You for Jesus and His excellent example of a life that demonstrates how to live in this weak human body, to Your honor and glory. Please help me overcome temptations and trust your enormous might in the face of difficult challenges. In Jesus's name, AMEN.

DAY FIFTY-THREE

JESUS, THE LIGHT OF THE WORLD

I am the light of the world. Whoever follows me will never walk in darkness, but will have the light of life.
John 8:12

Light cannot be hidden, for it draws attention to itself. When there is darkness around, we are all attracted to the light. This is the reason Jesus introduces Himself as the light. Jesus, as our Light, orders our exact steps and chases away the darkness.

On the way to Canaan, God led the Israelites with a pillar of fire. He did not leave them on their own. The presence of God's light doesn't mean that they took the easiest route. It instead implied that the light fully illuminated the road. Whenever Jesus is present in our lives, our paths are luminous.

PRAYER

Dear God, thank You for giving me the Light of Life in Jesus. I ask that You bring the light of Jesus into my life and guide me through this dark world without faltering. Help others find their way to You by using me to spread Your light to them. In Jesus's name, I pray, AMEN.

DAY FIFTY-FOUR

THE LORD'S GRACE IS SUFFICIENT

My grace is sufficient for you, for my power is made perfect in weakness.
2 Corinthians 12:9

In some ways, knowing that God is for you is all you need to know while facing your weaknesses. The past doesn't matter because God forgave and adopted you via Jesus Christ. His grace is sufficient for us. You are no longer a traitor to the King but a royal son or daughter. That is how God's grace works.

Our weakness and struggle open the door to the power of Christ, which calms storms, raises the dead, and allows ordinary men to walk on water.

PRAYER

Dear God, thank you for assuring me that Your grace is sufficient for all my needs. I know I'm weak, but I also know you use my weakness to demonstrate your power. Help me rejoice in my inabilities so that Your tremendous ability will be shown in my life. God, teach me that Your grace is all I need and that I cannot earn it through my efforts. May all I do, Lord and God, be to Your honor and glory. AMEN, in Jesus's name.

DAY FIFTY-FIVE

HUMBLE YOURSELF BEFORE THE LORD

Humble yourselves, therefore, under God's mighty hand,
that he may lift you up in due time.
1 Peter 5:6

All of us long to be acknowledged. We long to know that we are significant, and to have others know it, as well. That desire is not necessarily wrong. Every person desires to have some legitimate, God-honoring purpose, and a means to express it properly. Because we are made in God's image, the desire to be exalted is also built into us.

The Bible admonishes us to quit struggling to make greatness happen, rather we should trust God to exalt us at the right time and place as He sees fit. Our God is a good Father who loves us; He will do the best for us!

PRAYER

Dear God, help me develop a humility of heart and a graciousness of spirit. I pray for a humble spirit. Please help me understand I am not the source of my success, happiness, and prosperity. Keep me modest as I interact with others. I want others to see a reflection of You in me rather than a reflection of myself. Amen.

DAY FIFTY-SIX

WITH GOD ALL THINGS ARE POSSIBLE

Jesus looked at them and said, "With man this is impossible, but with God all things are possible.
Matthew 19:26

God is not at our bidding, but we are at his. Although it is true that God is always with his children and gives them strength, he does not guarantee that we will succeed in every venture.

When we use this verse incorrectly, we set ourselves up for frustration, doubt, and sorrow. God is all-powerful, but he does not give us the right to claim that power for whatever we want.

When Jesus prayed to his Father in the garden before he was taken to the cross, "all things are possible for you," he concluded by saying, "Yet not what I will, but what you will." The reality of the Father's absolute power compelled Jesus to submit to the Father's will.

PRAYER

Dear God, thank You for your flawless Word; for closing all the wrong doors and opening all the right ones. I know that with You, everything is possible! Nothing is impossible for You. Father, today I choose to stand in faith, trust and walk in every blessing You have in store for me. In Jesus's name, Amen.

DAY FIFTY-SEVEN

NEVER HESITATE TO DO GOOD WHEN YOU'RE OUGHT TO

If anyone, then, knows the good they ought to do and doesn't do it, it is sin for them.
James 4:17

The Bible is not only our guidebook for life and living, but it is also our spiritual level for truth. The primary purpose of a Christian should be to live the Christian life as God intended. The greatest challenge for a Christian is to challenge oneself to do the right thing.

Taking a shortcut may be a little profitable, and doing the right thing may take longer, but just trust the process, your reward is sure.

PRAYER

Dear God, thank You for the reality revealed in the book of James that when I know what is right but do not do it, I am sinning in Your eyes. Please accept my apologies for instances when I did nothing. Open my eyes to discover where and how I may help others. Give me affection for those who are close to me. In the name of Jesus, Amen.

DAY FIFTY-EIGHT

FEAR NOT, FOR GOD IS YOUR FORTRESS

Truly he is my rock and my salvation; He is my fortress; I will not be shaken.
Psalm 62:6

Life is full of ups and downs. But often, the most challenging place to be is in the middle. David wrote this Psalm when Saul was hunting for him. As he was running for his life, David concentrated his mind on what mattered most.

As David took refuge in caves and hillsides, he realized God was his refuge. In that cave, David made peace with God and declared in a song of worship that man can lie about him, hunt him, and try to take his crown, but he would trust in the Lord at all times.

We learn to trust God more when we pour out our hearts to Him and wait for Him to pave the way. We can put our faith in various things, including money, intellect, and talents. But nowhere is safer than with God, who created everything, understands everything, and has the power to fix anything.

PRAYER

Dear God, thank You for giving us rest. Fill us with eternal hope and serenity today as we throw our cares on You. Continue to teach us to rest in You, trust You, and realize that our ultimate hope is in You. In all these things, we pray, amen.

DAY FIFTY-NINE

FEAR NOT, FOR GOD IS YOUR FORTRESS

... give thanks in all circumstances; for this is God's will for you in Christ Jesus.
1 Thessalonians 5:18

What is a thankful heart? The word of God says, give thanks "in" all circumstances, not "for" all circumstances.

Being thankful is a blessed state of mind. It's powerful enough to alter the attitudes and the emotions of people who are in desperately hopeless situations.

If we can just thank God for being there for us at all times, that itself is a blessed attitude. Such an attitude will give thanks to God even in the middle of a storm with a strong trust that God will bring you back to the intended shore, safe and sound!

PRAYER

Dear God, I sincerely appreciate Your unfailing existence in my life; thank You, Father Lord. Today, I pray, help me grow in grace and thankfulness for all You've done for me. Please increase my gratitude and awareness of your presence today. Amen, in Jesus's name.

DAY SIXTY

TAKE DELIGHT IN THE LORD

Take delight in the Lord,
and he will give you the desires of your heart.
Psalm 37:4

We are all bent to admire our heroes. Whether it's an athlete, musician or an actor, we enjoy following their accomplishments. But God created us with the longing to admire all the wonders of who God is and His excellent greatness. Looking to a person to fill this God-given desire will never bring true delight or satisfaction.

When you delight in the excellencies of God, you will come to understand that everything about Him is the answer to your longings.

PRAYER

Dear God, thank you for desiring to bless me and shower me with the riches of your grace. Please forgive me for the times that I've taken delight in the wrong things. Dear Lord, kindly touch my heart to want Your will and assist me in keeping my eyes on Jesus and delighting in God's things. AMEN, I pray in Jesus's name.

DAY SIXTY-ONE
STAND BEFORE THE LORD

At that time the LORD set apart the tribe of Levi ... to stand before the LORD to minister and to pronounce blessings in his name.
Deuteronomy 10:8

The entire stadium stands in excitement when a goal is scored on a soccer field. We rise when an honored guest enters the room.

In ancient Israel, the tribe of Levi was set apart for another kind of standing. The Levites were chosen "to stand before the Lord to minister and to pronounce blessings in his name." This was a call to serve the Lord in the many duties required to help people worship God, and to share the good news of God's blessings for all.

So the Levites were in this way like the angels of heaven. The angel who came to announce the birth of John the Baptist later said, "I am Gabriel. I stand in the presence of God, and I have been sent to ... tell you this good news" (Luke 1:19).

God calls us to stand by putting on his armor so that we can "be strong in the Lord and in his mighty power." Our enemy, the devil, wants to knock us down, but in God's strength, we can "stand against the devil's schemes" (Ephesians 6:10-11), using God's gifts to honor our Lord in all we do.

PRAYER

Dear Father, thank You for Your unfailing love that I witness daily in every area of my life. Today, Father, please help me stand as a witness to Your goodness wherever I am. I need Your strength and grace to be a true child of God. Amen.

DAY SIXTY-TWO

BY THE SPIRIT OF THE MOST HIGH

So he said to me, This is the word of the Lord to Zerubbabel: 'Not by might nor by power, but by my Spirit,' says the Lord Almighty.
Zechariah 4:6

When life gets hard, we cannot overcome the many challenges, setbacks, and discouragements through our power or might, but only through the Spirit of God.

In other words, not by your strength, not by your mind, not by power, not by the resources you bring to the table, not by all of your abilities and talents and gifts combined. Not by any of those things. Apart from God we cannot successfully move forward in our life.

Everything that you do is not ultimately your strength, but God's strength and, every thought, word, and deed that we do is for his glory and can only happen by the power of his spirit in you. So this is why we pray. We pray to express our need for God. If we are not prayerful, then we must be prideful because prayer is the avenue God has given us among other things to express our need for Him.

PRAYER

Thank You, Heavenly Father, for the encouragement I get from God's Word, which is alive, well, and sharper than any two-edged sword. Thank You for empowering me to do Your work is not through my strength, cleverness, or wisdom but through Your Spirit, who lives inside me. Thank You, in Jesus's name, AMEN.

DAY SIXTY-THREE

GOD DETESTS PRIDE

*The fear of the LORD is to hate evil: pride, and arrogance,
and the evil way, and the forward mouth, do I hate.*
Proverbs 8:13 (KJV)

When we have a deep and a reverential relationship with God, we will love what He loves and hate what He hates. In the scriptures, we see God hates evil, which is defined as pride, arrogance, evil behavior, and vile speech. These are things that we should avoid.

God wants his people to be people of character — people of humility, moral behavior, and helpful speech. The true fear of the LORD will cause you to hate what God hates. You may want to tear every aspect of those things out of your life.

PRAYER

Father, forgive me of my pride and self-interest. Forgive me for my arrogance and heal my tongue. Let your Spirit mold me to be a person who is holy in word and deed, compassionate toward those in need, and freed from evil. To you, O LORD, be the glory in my life. In Jesus' name. Amen.

DAY SIXTY-FOUR

GOD GIVES RICHES

I will give you hidden treasures, riches stored in secret places, so that you may know that I am the LORD, the God of Israel, who summons you by name.
Isaiah 45:3

God orchestrated the release of the Israelites from bondage to Babylon through a Persian king named Cyrus. Interestingly, King Cyrus literally found treasures that the Jews had buried as they were taken into captivity. Like King Cyrus, who found treasures hidden in the darkness, you, too, can find treasures—hope in the unexpected places of darkness, those painful places of suffering where you would like not to be.

God has the power to intervene in your darkness. God is above time, space, and matter, and His existence is not dependent on anything outside of Himself. His ways are higher than your ways and His thoughts higher than your thoughts.

PRAYER

Father, I am thankful that my hardships are assisting me in growing and discovering God's bigger purpose, character development. Amen!

DAY SIXTY-FIVE

FOCUS ON WHAT PLEASES GOD

Set your affection on things above, not on things on the earth. **Colossians 3:2**

Our *affection* — that feeling of fondness or love — is to be set on things above and not on things on earth. So what does that really mean? It means we are to live with eternity in mind. Amid the daily ups and downs of life, our focus often is set on the day-to-day grind of life, our careers, our families, our friends, and our dreams and goals. This earthly focus makes it hard to retrain our thoughts to eternal things.

While there's nothing wrong with doing well for yourselves here on earth, ultimately you should also remember that you're not taking anything with you when you leave. As Christians, our citizenship is in heaven (Philippians 3:20). When we choose a heavenly mindset, rather than an earth-focused mindset, we have the peace that transcends all understanding (Phil. 4:7), the kind of peace that only God can give (John 14:27). Peace that can defeat the anxiety stirred up by even a smallest trigger.

PRAYER

Help me, Heavenly Father, to keep my heart fixed on Jesus and the magnificent everlasting inheritance You have provided for me and those who have trusted Jesus as Savior, I pray in Jesus's name. AMEN

DAY SIXTY-SIX

WORRY NOT

Can any one of you by worrying add a single hour to your life?
Matthew 6:27

Anxiety, worry, fret, distress, agitation, tension, and the irritability that we experience are natural human responses, and they affect your life, your decisions, and ultimately the direction of your life, especially when you are going through a tough season. However, the Scripture explains the key to living anxiety-free is to instead of focusing on trials, to turn your thoughts to prayer, petition, and thankfulness to God.

By choosing to trust God and follow His strategy for living rather than depending on the ever-changing, unpredictable, shaky systems of this world, you'll begin to see your anxiety and worry level disappear. Trusting God and praying will make a difference since it releases faith. This gives God the opportunity to move into your circumstances.

PRAYER

Dear Father, I admit that I am prone to worrying, but I see that this is folly and evidence of my lack of confidence in Your tremendous and valuable promises. May I rest in Your love, knowing that You will meet all my needs according to Your glorious riches! I pray in Jesus's name. AMEN!

DAY SIXTY-SEVEN

ALWAYS TRUST IN THE LORD

Though he slay me, yet will I trust in him: but I will maintain mine own ways before him.
Job 13:15

Job is going about his private affairs, unaware that he has suddenly become the focus of Satan's attention. Job's faith in God has become the object of a test by Satan, in which God is planning to pull the rug out from under Satan. When experience unpleasant circumstances, we often think it must be because God is angry with us. Yet this is a flawed way of looking at life. Your behavior might disappoint God, but He is fully aware of your shortcomings and your nature. Those things don't make God angry at you.

What God is teaching Job in this book is that living for today is not what it is all about. This is not why human existence is given to us; this life is school time, a time of preparation to get us ready for the real life that lies ahead. God uses these life situations to build your life to be a better person. Job came out of his situation with more trust, more faith, and more love for God.

PRAYER

Father in Heaven, help me recognize You are with me even in the most difficult of circumstances, and Your grace is sufficient no matter what pressures and issues I may encounter. Increase my confidence and hope in You and enable me to be firm amid adversity. I pray in Jesus's name, AMEN.

DAY SIXTY-EIGHT

HAVING AN ABSOLUTE CONVICTION IN CHRIST

If we are thrown into the blazing furnace, the God we serve is able to deliver us from it, and he will deliver us from Your Majesty's hand.
Daniel 3:17-18

It is common to hear of a person who had believed in God for a time but chose to walk away from God because God did not deliver them from something. One of the more common reasons is that the person prayed for either healing for a loved one, and God did not heal the person. You must decide in your heart to follow God regardless of whether He answers your prayers the way you desire. You have to trust that He is doing what is the best for you.

Make the choice not to bow down to any idols in this world. Worship God and God alone. Draw aside to the secret place where only you and God exist. This is the place where you declare, I have only You to trust, Oh God! And I will only bow before you!

PRAYER

Heavenly Father, please help me remain firm in faith even in the face of trials and tribulations. Help me completely trust in you. Thank you, Heavenly Father.

DAY SIXTY-NINE

LET YOUR FAITH BE STRONG

And being fully persuaded that, what he had promised, he
was able also to perform.
Romans 4:21

The Old Testament patriarch, Abraham was persuaded that whatever God promised He was faithful to perform for scripture declares Abraham never doubted at the promises of God.

Despite his old age and Sarah being barren, Abraham believed God was a promise keeper. He believed God would do what he promised.

A readiness to believe every promise implicitly, to obey every command in the Bible with no wavering, to stand perfect and complete in all the will of God, is how our faith will be strong. Clinging on the promises of God is contagious, it transfers to family, to people close to us, and eventually to the community. Faith in God is contagious!

PRAYER

Thank You, Heavenly Father, that I, like Abraham, have been justified by faith in the Lord Jesus Christ, my God, and Savior. Thank You I am welcomed in Christ and pronounced righteous - not for what I have done, but for believing in what Christ did on the Cross for me. May my life be a living testament to the truth of Christ's glorious gospel to everyone I encounter and may everything I do be done to God's glory, in Jesus's name and for His greater glory, AMEN.

DAY SEVENTY

TRUST GOD'S PROCESS

Therefore, know that the Lord your God, He is God, the faithful God who keeps covenant and mercy for a thousand generations with those who love Him and keep His commandments.
Deuteronomy 7:9

The word translated "faithful" is a participial form of the verb 'aman, from which we get the Greek word "amen." The Hebrew verb means "to stay," "to support," "to be firm," stressing the idea of utter dependability.

Commitment is not very common today. People break their word. God, on the other hand, always stays true to His word and has been faithful for all eternity. Faithfulness is not something God aspires to; it is an essential part of His character. When God makes a promise, He always keeps it.

We should know without a doubt that God who has adopted us as children has made us accepted in the Beloved. He has sealed us with His Holy Spirit, who has come to dwell within our mortal bodies, and has also given us an everlasting assurance that we are saved, sanctified, glorified, and have already been given eternal life.

PRAYER

Dear Father, I know you are forever amazing! You are a beautiful covenant-keeping God, and each day I want to know and love You more and more. Thank You for keeping Your promises in Your Word of Truth, I pray in Jesus's name. AMEN

DAY SEVENTY-ONE

SING A JOYFUL SONG UNTO THE LORD

I will sing to the LORD all my life; I will sing praise to my God as long as I live.
Psalm 104:33

Singing is such a wonderful gift! First, it is a gift from God to us, to help us express our joy, excitement, sorrow, and victory. Second, it is a gift from us to God, to help us communicate our respect, appreciation, love, and confidence in God. So let's sing, praising God for what he has done, proclaiming what he will do, and sharing what he is currently doing in our lives!

The words you sing should include thoughts that stir you to action and challenge you to worship the Lord for who He is. For its in worship, God captures your heart, and when He has your heart, He starts working on you.

PRAYER

Heavenly Father, I am grateful that You are my God, and I am Your child. May my thoughts and my heart's meditation be pleasant music in Your ears. How I worship You, for You alone deserve all honor and glory because You alone are the Lord of heaven and earth. O my soul, worship the Lord, and everything within me praise Your glorious name. Let all that has breath praise the Lord! AMEN.

DAY SEVENTY-TWO
BE THE GOOD MAN

A good man brings good things out of the good stored up in his heart, and an evil man brings evil things out of the evil stored up in his heart. For the mouth speaks what the heart is full of.
Luke 6:45

The heart is the center of human emotions. If we want to bear good fruit in life, we need to pay attention to what's on the inside, to our inner lives, to our hearts. The heart includes but is not limited to feelings. It is also the organ of discernment, judgment, and choosing.

If we long to live well, we should be conscious about the "fruit" of our lives and of our actions and words. The guarding of our hearts is of prime importance because producing 'fruits' are directly connected to the heart. True fruitfulness isn't putting on a show. Rather, it's an expression of a good heart formed by God as we engage in spiritual practices that help us be transformed by God's grace.

PRAYER

Father, assist us in avoiding harmful influences and actions linked with wickedness. Help us speak graciously and without bias and avoid what is not favorable in accordance with your holy rules. Do not let erroneous judgment cloud our judgment. People's attitudes and overall conduct reveal what is in their hearts. May we forgive and aid those who are fundamentally good, even if they make mistakes, and repent and avoid those who, with hypocritical sweetness, lure us into evil. In Jesus' name, we ask You to help us walk wisely in Your ways. Amen.

DAY SEVENTY-THREE
TESTING OF YOUR FAITH

Count it all joy, my brothers, when you meet trials of various kinds, for you know that the testing of your faith produces steadfastness. And let steadfastness have its full effect, that you may be perfect and complete, lacking in nothing.
James 1:2-4

At some point in your life, all of you have wanted to be somebody else. Some wanted to be Superman, some others a Spiderman. When you came to Christ, some of you wanted to be a David, Daniel, or Paul. As you learned about the history of the Church, you hoped to be Hudson Taylor, Martin Luther, Jonathan Edwards, or Amy Carmichael. But what you didn't consider is what it takes to become one of those men or women.

We look at the lives of others and think, "I'd like to be that Christlike." But what you don't consider is the pain, suffering, rigorous training and difficulties they had to experience in order to become that godly man or woman. Without pain, there's no gain. Endure the pain and make a difference.

The reason you're going through what you're going through is to receive the things you've been praying for. Often the thing that brings you the most pain is the very thing that will lead you to the most gain.

PRAYER

Heavenly Father, there are moments when I lament the hardships and tribulations that seem to pepper my journey through life. May I grow in my ability to see the many difficulties I endure as pure pleasure and the inevitable obstacles that will come my way as glorious chances to change. I pray to have the strength to face my daily challenges with joy, knowing that testing my faith will create perseverance and steadfastness. May I improve my reliance on You in good and challenging times. In Jesus's name, AMEN.

DAY SEVENTY-FOUR
WAIT ON THE LORD

I would have lost heart, unless I had believed that I would see the goodness of the Lord In the land of the living. Wait on the Lord; Be of good courage, and He shall strengthen your heart; wait, I say, on the Lord!
Psalm 27:13-14

Waiting and attempting to be patient and calm is one of the most challenging aspects of life. Especially when we are crying out to God, and He appears to be mute. We wonder if He is hearing us? Does He even exist? If that's the case, why is He not responding? I'm not sure why He appears mute, but I can assure you that He hears you, cares, and is present.

This is when faith enters the picture. Even when you can't see, you must trust. David places real value in the Lord's goodness. God's goodness motivates him to stay connected both with God and with the world around him, empowering him to wait patiently for the Lord's direction.

David is essentially saying here, "There is something SO GOOD about God that I know I'm going to see and experience personally. I am captivated by it. I want it. I will eagerly wait for it as long as necessary because it is so good it makes life worth living."

PRAYER

Heavenly Father, what a faithful God You are to all who trust in Your name. Thank You for the example of David, who reminds me that Your goodness and mercy lasts from generation to generation, and that all You have promised in Your Word is true and sure. In Jesus's name, AMEN!

DAY SEVENTY-FIVE

BE STILL

The Lord will fight for you; you need only to be still.
Exodus 14:14

God understood the struggles the Israelites were facing. He also knew the solutions to overcome those struggles. So He put the people where they needed to be, the right spots for victory. God parted the Red Sea letting the Israelites cross on dry ground. As the Egyptians followed in pursuit, God let the waters go, destroying the entire army. He won the battle for them.

No matter what kind of war you're in, God knows how to bring the victory. You are right where He wants you and you have everything you need to win because He is fighting for you.

PRAYER

Father, I praise You for Your numerous beautiful promises. Please forgive me when I lose sight of You and fall into disbelief. Keep my gaze fixed on Christ and the truth of Your Word. Help me rest in You and put all my problems in Your hands, allowing You to work in Your way and for Your glory. I pray in Jesus's name, AMEN.

DAY SEVENTY-SIX

GOD WILL NOT LET THE DEVIL WIN

Praise be to the LORD, the God of Israel, from everlasting to everlasting. Amen and Amen.
Psalm 41:13

This Psalms of David, Psalm 41 begins and ends with references to blessing. David starts with an initial statement on how God gets overwhelmed looking at someone who acts with love and compassion for the disadvantaged (Psalm 41:1–3). David also brings out how various spiritual activities are connected, like healing to forgiveness of sin, giving to motivation and so on.

What counts is not how much we give as the amount we retain. Giving and considering the poor may not be the only mark of a godly person, but it is a significant factor indeed.

PRAYER

Father, thank You for Your mercy. Thank You for giving me Your love, grace, and forgiveness instead of the punishment for my sins that I deserve. I soak in Your love. I soak in Your mercy to me. Help me see everything through the lens of Your mercy. Take away my heart of entitlement that makes demands on You and replace it with a heart of gratitude that is overwhelmed with all You have already given me in Your mercy alone. Thank You! Praise be to the Lord, from everlasting to everlasting! AMEN.

DAY SEVENTY-SEVEN

HANG ON, GOD IS IN CONTROL

The Lord blessed the latter part of Job's life more than the former part. He had fourteen thousand sheep, six thousand camels, a thousand yoke of oxen and a thousand donkeys.
Job 42:12

Man always opts for the strong, the successful, the victorious, the unbroken, in building their kingdoms; but God is the God of the unsuccessful, of those who have failed. We are not all like Job, but we all have Job's God. Though we may not have the kind of wealth Job had or go through the same process of loss as he went through, we have the same God with us, the God who will restore the loss maybe not in the same form, but in the same spirit, and with like design.

Heaven is filled with earth's broken lives; He can take the life crushed by pain or sorrow and make it into a vessel of honor. Whenever God restores something, He restores it to a place which is more valuable than what was lost.

PRAYER

Dear God, while I glance at the heavens and the incredible wonders You have made, I wonder what man is that You are aware of us, and yet You chose us. You chose me to be Your child. Let me surrender to Your Spirit's direction, understanding that nothing is good in me. I know You can do everything and that nothing You plan is impossible. Thank You, in Jesus's name, AMEN.

DAY SEVENTY-EIGHT

GOD IS CLOSE ENOUGH TO HEAR WHEN YOU CALL

The LORD is near to all who call on him, to all who call on him in truth.
Psalm 145:18

Have you been wondering lately where God is in your life? King David felt God had abandoned him. This is mentioned in several of his psalms. But notice the pattern? While he may start a Psalm lamenting that he feels God has forsaken him, by the end of the psalm he is praising God for His goodness and faithfulness!

When we feel like God can't hear us, it's at those times we really need to cry out to God! He hears! If you still don't feel God in your life, don't be afraid to come to Him. God knows your deepest thoughts and the desires of your heart. No matter how long it's been since you've truly felt God's presence; please know that calling out to Him is the solution. God doesn't push us away. He loves us; He pursues us, and He wants us to grow in our relationship with Him. Admitting that we need God's help isn't a sign of weakness; instead, it's expressing a desire to know God better.

PRAYER

Lord, we believe that when we pray and meditate on Your Holy Word; we have a deep relationship with You that profoundly influences our lives. Since You are a trustworthy God, we must walk beside You, and Your Holy Word includes all your promises to your people. You bring calm and safety to everyone who seeks Your presence, for You will never desert us. In Jesus' name, AMEN.

DAY SEVENTY-NINE
GOD HEALS

For he had one only daughter, about twelve years of age, and she lay a dying. But as he went the people thronged him.
Luke 8:42-44

The unnamed woman came for healing. She received much more than that. Jesus refused to allow the woman to receive an anonymous miracle. Instead, he had her come forward and then praised her faith and dismissed her to live in peace. She was not only healed; she was praised! In her fear, she ventured out in faith and received a double blessing.

Healing is not necessarily a deliverance from the physical sickness. Sometimes it can look like acceptance, belonging, and getting connected. Sometimes healing looks like not letting fear have a hold in your life. Love looks like a touch from someone else in a moment of shame, hopelessness, or deep pain to draw us out and remind us we are loved and called children of God.

PRAYER

Dear God, O LORD God, may my faith be as bold and as unrelenting as this woman's faith. Stir me to courage and action. In Jesus' name, I pray. Amen.

DAY EIGHTY
PRAY WITHOUT CEASING

And pray in the Spirit on all occasions with all kinds of prayers and requests. With this in mind, be alert and always keep on praying for all the Lord's people.
Ephesians 6:18

After detailing the parts of God's armor, Paul adds another crucial component of spiritual warfare: Prayer. This is not spiritual armor, yet it is necessary for victory in spiritual conflicts. Why?

Prayer ties us to God's strength, which is required to combat spiritual foes. Our prayers should not be about our thoughts or wishes but rather be in obedience to God. Just as a soldier's equipment is made for a worldly fight, a Christian's equipment is designed for spiritual warfare, and Prayer is our most powerful weapon.

PRAYER

Dear Father, You have blessed me with the priceless gift of prayer. Help me embrace my life and prayer with a sense of total reliance on You. May I be watchful and diligent in all my prayers. In the mighty name of Jesus. AMEN

DAY EIGHTY-ONE
REFLECT ON GOD'S WORK

I will remember the deeds of the Lord;
yes, I will remember your miracles of long ago.
Psalm 77:11

Why is it crucial to reflect on God's work in your life?

The powerful works that God has done in the past encourage us to hold on to our faith, even in difficult times, because we know God has been faithful in the past and will continue to be faithful in the future. God's actions in the past can serve as a source of hope and encouragement for us in the present.

What you remember of God's leading in the past functions as a means of information for the present and helps shape your future.

PRAYER

Dear Father, thank you for Your limitless miracles and blessings I get to witness constantly in my life. Dear God, help me remember what You have done for me in the past whenever I am stuck in life's struggles. I bless Your holy name, Amen.

DAY EIGHTY-TWO
BE OBEDIENT

If you are willing and obedient, you will eat the good things of the land.
Isaiah 1:19

God can provide for our needs and bless us with abundance. This is a promise of hope and comfort, reminding us that no matter what challenges we may face, God can provide for us and bless us with all that we need.

Obeying God's commands may not always be easy, and there may be times when it requires sacrifice or discomfort. But the rewards of obedience far outweigh any temporary hardships. As we seek to follow God's will and obey His commands, God aligns us with His will and purpose and helps us experience His protection, extraordinary provision, and favor.

PRAYER

Dear Lord, please grant me a heart that is willing and obedient to Your commands. Oh Lord, count me among those who will partake of the produce of the land I am on. I give thanks to You for hearing my prayers. In the powerful name of Jesus, amen.

DAY EIGHTY-THREE

GOD WILL FINISH WHAT HE STARTED

The LORD will vindicate me; your love, LORD, endures forever— do not abandon the works of your hands.
Psalm 138:8

The Bible tells us that God has a plan for our lives. You are vital to God's plan on the earth. However, the Bible doesn't always spell out exactly what we're to do and when. We don't get the whole plan for our life laid out at once. We discover it by getting close to God and walking out His plan step by step. He's there to lead you and guide you through life.

Let us hold on to these promises and trust in his faithfulness, knowing that He will complete the good work that He began in us.

PRAYER

Father, please forgive me and assist me in rising. So that I might walk, jog, and run in Your ways, fill me with Your Spirit. I'm grateful for Your unwavering affection. As You fulfill Your plans for my life, let my life praise You. In Jesus' name, AMEN.

DAY EIGHTY-FOUR

GOD, THE FATHER OF LIGHT

*Every good and perfect gift is from above, coming down
from the Father of the heavenly lights, who does not change
like shifting shadows.*
James 1:17

Is God tempting you when you go through trials? By no means! God is the absolute Creator of all that is good, and He will always be characterized by his goodness, both regarding his character and regarding his relentless desire to give good gifts to his children.

While God is indeed a giver of good gifts, James has strong words for those who ask God for things with the wrong motives. *"You ask and you do not receive,"* he says, *"because you ask wrongly, to spend it on your passions."* (James 4:3, ESV) James also warns us to ask with trust in God's character, not doubting his goodness: *"Ask in faith, with no doubting...for* [the person who doubts] *must not suppose that he will receive anything from the Lord; he is a double-minded man, unstable in all his ways"* (James 1:7-8, ESV).

PRAYER

Dear Heavenly Father, I thank and praise You that Your love and grace are unchanging and our ever-present help in these trying times in a world filled with uncertainty and challenges. I thank

You, dear Lord, that You are my unchanging God, my unchange-able Provider, and the Lover of my soul even when my faith wanes and my love grows chilly. In Jesus's name, Amen. Praise be to Your holy name.

DAY EIGHTY-FIVE

POSSESS THE FEAR OF GOD

The fear of the Lord is the beginning of wisdom,
and knowledge of the Holy One is understanding.
Proverbs 9:10

Wisdom starts with a God centered view of the world. That is so key. Because wisdom flows from seeing God for who He is and responding to Him appropriately. Much of the wisdom in the world doesn't spring from a God centeredness.

Ultimate wisdom is found only when we intentionally humble ourselves before our incredible God, giving Him the reverence and worship, He deserves. For, the fear of God is the greatest antidote against the fear of man.

PRAYER

Heavenly Father, give me an understanding heart in awe for Your great and glorious majesty and a growing knowledge of my Lord and Savior, Jesus Christ. The more I comprehend Your eternal character and the unrivaled qualities to Your praise and glory, the more I will know Him and the power of His Resurrection. The more I will fellowship in His suffering and pain. In the name of Jesus, Amen.

DAY EIGHTY-SIX

SEEK TO HELP THE NEEDY

And I have been a constant example of how you can help those in need by working hard. You should remember the words of the Lord Jesus, 'It is more blessed to give than to receive.

Acts 20:35

The measure of a life well-lived is not the amount we have gained, but the difference we have made in the lives of others.

True greatness is not found in what we have achieved for ourselves, but in what we have done to serve and uplift others.

The core of faithful living is making one's time and possessions accessible to serve God and others.

God loved us so much that He gave. He gave His only begotten Son, Jesus Christ to save the world. Generosity starts from the cross, the center of God's love. With such a love, generosity not only is possible but inevitable. Our giving is but a reflex of God's giving.

PRAYER

Dear LORD Jesus, remind us of the blessings we received and help us give generously. Amen.

DAY EIGHTY-SEVEN

BLESSINGS FOR THE SAVED

And we know that all things work together for good to them that love God, to them who are called according to his purpose. **Romans 8:28**

Romans 8:28 is a promise for believers. Real believers. Those who are living for Christ. The most important truth here is that the total of all events works for good. There's a difference between saying "each thing by itself is good" and "all things work together for good." The difference is tremendous.

God's purpose in your life is to make you more like Jesus. The "good" here is not about giving you better circumstances—as if every bad event will automatically lead to a greater one later on. The "good" of Romans 8 is God making you a better *you*—that is, more like Jesus.

PRAYER

Father, sometimes I can't understand how You can bring beauty from the ashes of my life. I struggle to trust You with the broken pieces. You say in Your Word that without faith it is impossible to please You, and I want to please You. I want to trust You. I want You to make me more like Jesus and use my trials for my good and Your glory. Help me believe the promise of Romans 8:28. In the strong name of Jesus, I ask. Amen.

DAY EIGHTY-EIGHT

FULFILLING YOUR CALLING

*And remember that thou was a servant in the land of
Egypt, and that the LORD thy God brought thee out
thence through a mighty hand and by a stretched out arm:
therefore the LORD thy God commanded thee to keep the
Sabbath day.*
Deuteronomy 5:15

When God told the Israelites to keep Sabbath, He added an important reason; to remember that they were slaves in Egypt. In Egypt, they'd been forced to work ceaselessly without basic privilege. Once freed, they were to give themselves a whole day each week to ensure they remembered the goodness of God.

A person who honors God this way is content because in rhythms of rest we discover our time is full of the holiness of God.

PRAYER

Thank You, Heavenly Father, help me understand that a day spent in Your presence is the most valuable moments of the entire week. I am thus investing not only for my life here on earth but also for eternity. AMEN.

DAY EIGHTY-NINE
GOD REMAINS FAITHFUL

"The Lord will rescue me from every evil attack and will bring me safely to his heavenly kingdom. To him be glory forever and ever.
2 Timothy 4:18

The apostle Paul imitated Christ as he walked in his Christian life. Early in his life he persecuted Christians. Later, he experienced persecution, suffering many times for Christ's sake. This suffering did not deter him from following Christ, neither did it discourage his spiritual son Timothy from following Christ. Instead, Paul, in the midst of his struggles, encouraged Timothy to keep true to the Lord and assured him that the Lord would rescue him from every evil attack.

It is a blessing to have good examples to encourage us that whatever we are suffering right now or whatever suffering will be in the future; we are not alone. The key point that Paul tells Timothy is to remain joyful in the presence of God because He is the God who rescues us.

God does not stop at rescuing us; the purpose of that rescue is to encourage us to keep trusting Him and to have fellowship with Him.

PRAYER

Heavenly Father, just as Paul has urged us all to cling to the unbreakable truth of God's Word. We are grateful to You, Father, for keeping Your promise to deliver Your children from all evil deeds and safely bring us home to our heavenly inheritance in Christ. AMEN. To You be the eternal acclaim and glory.

DAY NINETY

DWELL IN GOD'S WORDS

I will meditate in thy precepts and have respect unto thy ways.
Psalm 119:15

The *'precepts'* are God's good rules for your conduct and behavior. So the challenge here is not about resolving to meditate upon God's Word as a spiritual and intellectual exercise like it is in several religions. Instead, it is about meditating in order to better shape your life to the design and pattern that God wants it to be.

Meditation, therefore, is how you fix your eyes upon God's ways and also prepare your heart to walk in them.

PRAYER

Dear Father, thank You for Your Word. Prepare me to be confronted by the Word of God, to overthrow my patterns of thought and behavior that are against Your Word.. Jesus, be praised, AMEN.

DAY NINETY-ONE

DO NOT NEGLECT THE GATHERING OF THE SAINTS

Again I say unto you, That if two of you shall agree on earth as touching anything that they shall ask, it shall be done for them of my Father which is in heaven. (KJV)
Matthew 18:19-20

The expression of the power of Jesus Christ is never fully seen in an individual Christian but only in the company of other Christians who gather with the same purpose. That purpose is to glorify God.

This is the simplest form of church, where two or three gather in Jesus's name. Individual Christians cannot fully reflect Jesus Christ. It is only when two or three, or two or three hundred, or two or three thousand are gathered in His name that the power of Jesus is fully manifested in this life.

This means we can never fully know Jesus Christ and can never experience His power unless we know Him in relation to a fellow Christian.

PRAYER

Heavenly Father, help me love the fellowship of your saints, because there is power in gathering together. In Jesus' name! AMEN.

DAY NINETY-TWO
GOD'S PROMISE

Through these he has given us his very great and precious promises, so that through them you may participate in the divine nature, having escaped the corruption in the world caused by evil desires.
2 Peter 1:4

God made us to be like Him in character. God wants us to participate in His divine nature which will enable us to be ready for the second coming of Jesus Christ.

Everything in our world is subject to corruption and decay, except us — those of us whose lives are united with Jesus! The true and the great promise from God is the promise of eternal life. Our response to this promise is to follow Christ wholeheartedly!

PRAYER

Thank You, Heavenly Father, that I now share in Christ's divine character as a result of Your grace and my confidence in Him. Thank You for the many precious promises found in the Word of truth for myself and all believers. I pray Your will for my life will be accomplished to Your honor and glory. Jesus, be praised, AMEN.

DAY NINETY-THREE
DRAW NIGH TO GOD

Draw nigh to God, and he will draw nigh to you. Cleanse your hands, ye sinners; and purify your hearts, ye double minded.
James 4:8

Feed your relationship with God. Dwelling in His Word, spending time in prayer, doing what God wants you to do are the ways you can grow in your relationship with Him. Ask God to reveal scriptures to you that will help you understand and deal with the things you're currently struggling with.

You'll be amazed at what He will show you, if you'll be open to letting Him speak to you.

More than anything God wants a living dynamic relationship with you. So let this time help you feed your relationship with God with things like growing closer to Him and getting into the word. The things God speaks to you about now may impact you for the rest of your life.

PRAYER

Lord, I desire to cultivate a peaceful mind toward You, have a pure heart, and keep my hands clean before You. Keep my eyes and ears open to hear Your voice, and keep my heart available to only You. I ask in the name of Jesus, Amen.

DAY NINETY-FOUR
KEEP LEARNING

Let the wise hear and increase in learning, and the one who understands obtain guidance.
Proverbs 1:5

A wise man never stops learning. He will hear things throughout his entire life and will continue learning from what he hears. Wisdom is acquired by the ears, not the mouth. You have two ears, but one mouth. You should be swift to hear and slow to speak.

Hearing and learning are not just about gathering a group of facts. The refer to when a person has insight due to the facts they know. This kind of learning leads someone to have insight and to be astute to what God is doing and saying. It means we can discern between good and evil and between knowing God and not knowing Him. When we increase in learning, we are not just increasing in the amount of knowledge we have. We are increasing in our ability to discern what God is speaking.

PRAYER

Heavenly Father, I pray I will always be humble enough to keep hearing what You are trying to teach me every day of my life. May I never reach a stage where I say, I know everything. In the name of Jesus, I ask. Amen.

DAY NINETY-FIVE
ALWAYS FORGIVE

And when you stand praying, if you hold anything against anyone, forgive them, so that your Father in heaven may forgive you your sins.
Mark 11:25

Faith in God and pride can never travel together. Pride considers itself always 'right' and has no need to forgive. That kind of thinking is like a mountain standing just against you. All you can see is the big mountain looming before you, and the mountain blocks everything God has for your life. Pride has a blinding affect and blocks you from seeing beyond where you are stuck.

But you have the power to remove the mountain when you forgive those who have offended you. Pride stops us from forgiving one another, but when you surrender your pride and let go of your need to be right, your faith can grow, and the mountain will disappear.

PRAYER

Father, Thank You for the forgiveness that is mine in Jesus Christ. Teach me to extend this forgiveness to those around me. In Jesus's name!

DAY NINETY-SIX

THE LORD WILL ESTABLISH YOU

After you have suffered for a little while, the God of all grace, who called you to His eternal glory in Christ, will Himself perfect, confirm, strengthen and establish you.
1 Peter 5:10

True spiritual growth begins in the places where we don't have things our way and we can't do anything about it. In these hard places, God grows you spiritually and molds you to be a better vessel for Him.

The process could be tough, but God will cover you with His grace. He is "the God of all grace," including the infinite, inexhaustible stores of future grace that we will need to endure to the end.

Faith in that future grace, strengthened by the memory of past grace, is the key to enduring on the narrow and hard road that leads to an established life.

PRAYER

Loving Father, we come to You today because we need You. We need You to help us discern the season. We want to know when to wait on God and when to act. Help us remember our sufferings are only for a while. Lord, teach us to be patient in waiting and to learn to live in the season we are in. In Jesus' name, Amen!

DAY NINETY-SEVEN

DO NOT HESITATE TO ASK FOR PRAYER

Is anyone among you sick? Then he must call for the elders of the church and they are to pray over him, anointing him with oil in the name of the Lord.
James 5:14

Prayer is a great privilege for a Christian. It grants to you an audience at the throne of grace, for mercy to find help in time of need. The book of James begins and ends with the "prayer of faith."

First, James warns against being a double-minded Christian. He speaks about praying with doubt in your hearts. At the end of his letter, James writes about the effective, fervent prayer of the righteous man. This prayer has its roots in trusting God and believing His Word.

We are not only encouraged to pray for ourselves and others, but we are also instructed to ask for prayer when we are in need.

PRAYER

Help me, Heavenly Father, to remember that You are the Great Physician, completely capable of healing. Forgive me for the times I doubted You and attempted to solve my problems alone. Give me a humble heart and strengthen my faith in You. In Jesus' name, I pray. AMEN.

DAY NINETY-EIGHT

THE GIFT OF THE HOLY SPIRIT

*The Spirit is God's guarantee that he will give us
the inheritance he promised and that he has purchased us
to be his own people. He did this so we would praise and
glorify him.*
Ephesians 1:14

God is a promise keeper! He gave us a down payment, a deposit, so we could be sure of our inheritance and look forward to the full realization of our salvation. He gave us the Holy Spirit.

Eventually, God will buy us out of the slavery to our mortal bodies and redeem us into our eternal bodies that will not grow old or decay. We won't need the deposit; we will have the full inheritance. Until then, until we go to Him, God makes His home within our mortal bodies through the Spirit.

PRAYER

Heavenly Father, Thank You for sending your blessed and promised Spirit to live in me and remind me where my home truly is. Thank You for not making me wait to experience Your presence. Thank You for giving me "a foretaste of glory divine." Until the day I see You face-to-face, I want to honor Your presence in my mortal body by living a life that is pure, holy, and a blessing to others. In Jesus' name I pray. Amen.

DAY NINETY-NINE

HOLY SPIRIT OUR COUNSELLOR

But the Advocate, the Holy Spirit, whom the Father will send in my name, will teach you all things and will remind you of everything I have said to you.
John 14:26

Sometimes we might think faith was easier for the disciples because they could walk and talk and eat with Jesus in person. On the night before He was crucified, Jesus told his disciples that they were going to receive the Holy Spirit.

The Spirit is a person, as fully God as the Father and the Son. The Spirit of God comes to dwell within believers, indicating that a new level of intimacy between God and his people is possible.

PRAYER

Father, make Your Spirit known to me. Help me sense Your presence and to hear Your voice in my life. This I ask, in the name of Jesus, AMEN.

DAY ONE HUNDRED

THANKFULNESS

Give thanks to the God of heaven. His love endures forever.
Psalm 136:26

Thank-ful-ness. The term itself implies that our thankfulness should be abundant. We should be grateful for the food we eat, clothes to cover our nakedness, homes to live in, money to spend, and much more.

Because of these things, we give thanks to the Lord of the Universe. He provides food for all creatures (v. 25), and He also does much more. Give thanks to the Lord of Lords because his love for us is steadfast in Jesus Christ in every way, every day. And because we have received the Lord's everlasting love, our cup is always overflowing.

PRAYER

Dear Father, as I have learned from your book always to praise you, I kneel in deepest humility today to thank you for what you have done for me, what you are still doing for me, and what you will do in the future. Please help me constantly praise you regardless of my circumstances. Amen.

DAY ONE HUNDRED AND ONE

DELIVERANCE STARTS WITHIN

But I trust in you, LORD; I say, "You are my God." My times
are in your hands; deliver me from the hands of my enemies,
from those who pursue me.
Psalm 31:14-15

God's deliverance starts with me. The first deliverance is always the defeat of our old lifestyle. The real deliverance is always the change inside a person. Inside change transforms how we live our life. God will break us, shatter our strength, and bring us to our knees.

God uses the things that seem to destroy to deliver us. We should not run from the opportunities God uses for our deliverance. The more we embrace such opportunities, the more we will see God working in us and for us.

PRAYER

Loving Father, I have sought refuge in You, as David did, and I trust in Your steadfast Word and never-failing promises. For the sake of Your good name, I beg You release me from the hardships I am experiencing now. Please grant me the strength to persevere. AMEN, I pray in Jesus's name.

DAY ONE HUNDRED AND TWO

CLOSELY FOLLOWING THE WORD OF GOD

*Before I was afflicted, I went astray, but now I keep
your word.*
Psalm 119:67

When we follow the Word of God, it will confront us and overthrow our pattern of thinking and living. It will disturb our security, undermine our complacency, and topple our patterns of thought and behavior.

The Word of God can be seen as the straight edge which shows our crookedness. The straight edge of Scripture exposes the crookedness of our thinking.

PRAYER

Thank You, Heavenly Father, for Your protection and the treasures concealed within Your Word. May Your Word become my daily sustenance and life-support. Your Word helps can keep me from the evil one and enables me to live a life pleasing to You. AMEN, in Jesus's name.

DAY ONE HUNDRED AND THREE

COUNT ON GOD TO DIRECT YOUR PLANS

A man's heart plans his way, But the LORD directs his steps.
Proverbs 16:9

The plans we make should be specific and as detailed as possible for everything. We should visualize our plans, see them happening. We should pray over our plans intensely till we see God intervening, either working with us or till we see God scrapping our plan and replacing it with His.

The most important lesson I have learned is to trust God in every circumstance. It's easier said than done. His delays are not always denials. Those are the times God is asking me to lay aside my planning to have things according to His way.

PRAYER

Dear GOD, thank You for allowing me to make plans while also giving me the delightful confidence that You are the One Who governs my actions and directs my steps.

DAY ONE HUNDRED AND FOUR

MAKE USE OF EVERY OPPORTUNITY

*Look carefully then how you walk, not as unwise but
as wise,*
Ephesians 5:15

God sends several opportunities our way. Some look so insignificant and negligible. But God knows how those opportunities fit into the greater plan of God for us. When we accept those opportunities, new ways open up.

For David, the killing of the giant Goliath changed his life exponentially. However, Goliath didn't come to David. David was obeying his dad's instruction to take lunch for his brothers. On the other hand, if opportunity doesn't come our way, we can always create a way. Giving is one such way. It opens up doors of opportunity. The best definition of opportunity is 'a set of circumstances that makes it possible to do something.' Giving creates our circumstances.

PRAYER

Dear Father, provide me with your divine knowledge, which includes vigilance to issues and opportunities, avoidance of addictions, and sensitivity to know the best approach to bless others based on their needs. I pray in Jesus's name.

DAY ONE HUNDRED AND FIVE

LIVE WITH ETERNITY IN FOCUS!

For my thoughts are not your thoughts, neither are your ways my ways ,declares the Lord.
Isaiah 55:8-9

Thoughts cause outcomes. The things that God thinks and purposes are much different from what we think and purpose. Therefore, because His thoughts are different, the results of his thoughts are different.

When God calls us to think as He thinks, He is asking us to have eternity in perspective for every small and big action we do. That is to live with eternity in focus.

PRAYER

Dear God, thank You for this day and the days to come. Lord I pray, help me stay focused on Your path and strengthen me so I will remain focused till the end.

DAY ONE HUNDRED AND SIX

GOD WHO LOVES TO COMMUNE WITH US

Yes, my soul, find rest in God; my hope comes from him.
Psalm 62:5

In the Old Testament, we see the Israelites in the wilderness looking to God for food. God provided them with manna, which was to be collected as per their need every day. This was how God wanted to commune with them. When they came to collect their daily share of manna, they didn't just collect food. They also entered a time when God communed with them. God saw a need and wanted to not only provide for them but spend time with them within their need. God could have provided the manna that stayed fresh. Instead, He chose to have the Israelites come to Him every morning.

So every morning, they got an opportunity to refresh their perspective about who their God was. These were also moments when they could realign their hearts toward God. And finally, they would walk away with a renewed spirit. This perfectly explains why we may have to face the same issue over and over in our life.

PRAYER

What a delight to realize that all my hope comes from You, Loving Father. My stability, love, pleasure, and happiness are grounded in the Lord Jesus Christ. Thank You, Father, for allowing me to rest in You at all hours of the day and night. AMEN, I pray in Jesus's name.

DAY ONE HUNDREED AND SEVEN

REMEMBERING WHAT GOD HAS DONE

When they had all had enough to eat, he said to his disciples, 'Gather the pieces that are left over. Let nothing be wasted. '
John 6:12

Remembering what God has done is encouraging. Every one of us has many memories. Some are stories of struggles and pain, others of joy and celebration.

Each of them are important because they are part of the story God is writing. They are part of what has shaped us into who we are today.

Our faith is strengthened when we remember God's works in our lives, both small and big. A strengthened faith results in praise that comes more easily and prayers that flow more readily. In our remembering, we are ultimately, better equipped to strengthen the faith of others and glorify God.

PRAYER

Dear God, please allow me to reap the benefits of Your magnificent labour once I have stepped out in trust. You can move mountains, heal diseases, and achieve feats I cannot grasp or envision. You are indeed mighty Lord.

DAY ONE HUNDRED AND EIGHT

JESUS HELPS US TO PROGRESS IN LIFE

For everyone who asks receives; the one who seeks finds;
and to the one who knocks, the door will be opened.
Matthew 7:7-8

Sometimes we are unsure of what we want in life or how to attain the goals we have set for ourselves. It's not that getting to know Jesus changes what we want, it's just that knowing Him ignites the desire in us to progress in life. Things we wanted to do all along and had been trying so hard to do on our own can't be done without Him.

- Ask — God to be your Lord and Savior
- Seek — Him and His righteousness
- Knock — on the door that God has ready to open

It's only through Jesus that we can know which door God is ready to open.

PRAYER

Thank You, Heavenly Father, for clearly laying forth the principles and practices that should rule our lives as we die to ourselves and live for God. Thank You that my salvation depends not on what I have done but on what Christ has done for me. May I pray according to Your will, seek to develop in the grace and understanding of the Lord Jesus, and submit to the Holy Spirit's leadership and direction. AMEN, I pray in Jesus's name.

DAY ONE HUNDRED AND NINE

GOD IS THERE TO PICK US UP

For I am the LORD your God who takes hold of your right hand and says to you, Do not fear; I will help you.
Isaiah 41:13

We all fall from time to time and need help getting back up. God is always there, no matter how many times we fall. Falling is not the problem. The problem is getting back up. God will be there to pick us up. God always helps us in the way that we need help and does what is best for us. He will give us the most appropriate help at the most appropriate time. The right way, the right time, the right help, the right amount.

Proverbs 24:16 says, "For a just man falleth seven times, and riseth up again: but the wicked shall fall into mischief." For the one who is doing right, failure is not the end of the road. God is willing to lift us up again.

PRAYER

Dear Heavenly Father, You are trustworthy. You keep blessing me. You never abandon me. I pray for You to be present with me throughout the day today. Your word promises to hold my hand and orders me to "fear not," so please assist me throughout the day.

DAY ONE HUNDREED AND TEN

BUT GOD!

You intended to harm me, but God intended it for good to accomplish what is now being done, the saving of many lives.
Genesis 50:20

The word for "meant" comes from a Hebrew word that supposes a process of extended thinking and planning with a clear purpose in mind.

The intention of Joseph's brothers could have not been good when they sold him into slavery. But God allowed the evil plannings and doings of his brothers to turn them into a blessing for many, including Joseph's own family.

God's sovereignty has exciting implications for our lives. Evil never thwarts God's divine purposes for us, never. God is sovereign over all the events of our life, even when evil people act contrary to His will. Because we all carry something of God within us, something that this world needs, our wisdom, our love, our skills, the enemy will try to neutralize us by muting our influence. But God has already worked out the exit for us to come out of the mess. We need only trust Him.

PRAYER

Lord, guard me against evil, and I hope that when challenges and sufferings come my way, I can trust you implicitly like Joseph. Help me rest in the reality of Your Word, knowing that You control everything. Thank You for Your unfailing grace, no matter what I encounter. AMEN, in Jesus's name.

DAY ONE HUNDRED AND ELEVEN

GOD REVEALS HIS NAME!

The name of the LORD is a strong tower; the righteous run to it and are safe.
Proverbs 18:10

The moments of life when we faced larger problems are the times when experienced God in bigger ways! Walking away from God just because the situation of life is hard to bear, is like walking away from the victory stand moments before the race is to be won.

In the case of Moses, God equipped him for the greater task just because he had recognized God as Adonai. God doesn't always call the equipped but always equips the called. God reveals His name to every person according to the purpose of God in their lives. To Abraham, it was Jehovah Jireh and to Moses it was Adonai.

PRAYER

Thank you, LORD, for making Your name available to me. This day, I pray in Your name for safety, mercy, grace, and favor. I thank You as I live because every arrow and every strategy from the adversary is met by a defense from You. I live with the assurance that as long as I am in You; I am protected. Thank You, my father and God; I have prayed in Jesus's powerful name. Amen.

DAY ONE HUNDRED AND TWELVE

THE JUST SHALL LIVE BY FAITH

Now faith is the substance of things hoped for, the evidence of things not seen.
Hebrews 11:1

Faith is an essential requirement of life that keeps our hope alive and keeps us from being shaken when faced with trials. The stronger our faith in God is, the stronger our hope will be. Faith is the most potent force in the universe. It opens impossible doors and is the master key to a world of good reports. (Hebrews 11:2)

Without faith, our life will be full of struggles, and our hope and confidence will be cast off. Faith gives value to our destiny. Stand firm on the word of God and trust every word that proceeds from the mouth of God. Romans 1:17 tells us *"For in it the righteousness of God is revealed from faith to faith; as it is written, 'The just shall live by faith.'"*

PRAYER

Loving Father, sometimes I doubt Your Word and question Your promises, wishing I had some concrete 'proof' of Your love for me, and yet Your Word gives me all the affirmation of this absolute reality I need. For Your Word and promises are sure. Your faithfulness stretches beyond the limits of time and space. Thank

You for the gift of faith, and I hope that my loving trust in You and the reality of Your Word grow stronger in my heart daily. I wish to please You in all I say, do, and am. AMEN, I pray in Jesus's name.

DAY ONE HUNDRED AND THIRTEEN

CONTROLLING THE TONGUE

Those who guard their lips preserve their lives, but those who speak rashly will come to ruin.
Proverbs 13:3

Communication is an essential—and powerful—part of life. The way you use and choose words defines who you are. How we use words touches us as well as those around us. That's why our words should be consistent with our testimony. Our words can harm our witness for the Lord. Christians with loose tongues are inconsistent at their best and hypocritical at their worst.

The only way to protect our tongue is to protect our hearts. Jesus said that the things that defile us spring from the heart. Proverbs 4:23 calls the heart the "wellspring of life." The mouth speaks what the heart gives it to say.

PRAYER

Take hold of my words, Heavenly Father. Please assist me in thinking before I speak. Help me talk in a way that builds rather than destroys. I want my words to honor You rather than be used by the enemy. Amen.

DAY ONE HUNDRED AND FOURTEEN

WE CAN WIN THE BATTLE

For our struggle is not against flesh and blood, but against the rulers, against the authorities, against the powers of this dark world.
Ephesians 6:12

The reason for all physical manifestations of struggle is a spiritual reality. A problem with another person is really a spiritual problem. A problem with the effects of a fallen world, especially when it concerns hostility to the gospel or with God's way of living, is not truly a struggle against the flesh and blood manifestations of those problems.

Just as in any military strategy, it is fatal to underestimate the enemy's strength. We need to understand that all darkness and struggle have one source, Satan, and his mysterious hierarchy of demonic principalities who have been allowed temporarily to cause trouble in this present darkness.

So, our battle is a spiritual one; the spiritual weapons of prayer, godliness, and the truth revealed by the Holy Spirit and the Word of God are our defense against it. As we use these weapons, we also have the grace of God to our advantage. Every battle can be won this way.

PRAYER

Thank You, Heavenly Father, that Christ Jesus has triumphed over sin, Satan, and the demonic forces in this world's darkness. Help me recognize that I can only beat the world's spiritual adversaries via Christ. Thank You for equipping me to live a triumphant life in Christ through the Word of God, prayer, and praise and for abiding in Christ and He in me. AMEN, I pray in Jesus's name.

DAY ONE HUNDRED AND FIFTEEN

PRAYER CHANGES OUR PERSPECTIVE

But when you pray, go into your room, close the door and pray to your Father, who is unseen. Then your Father, who sees what is done in secret, will reward you.
Matthew 6:6

We never know how God will answer our prayers. Most often, the answer to our prayer may not change our life or the circumstances, but it will change us. Every time God moves to answer our prayer, He will get us involved. Because God knows us so well, He also knows the motive of our prayers. If we are true intercessors, we must be ready to participate in God's work on behalf of the people we pray for.

Prayers should not be used for selfish gain. Every prayer should encourage us to see changes in our perspective and expansion of the Kingdom of God. Prayers are how we keep connected to our Father in heaven. The more we are connected to Him, we see His heart, and we understand what His response will be.

PRAYER

Keep me, Heavenly Father, from the temptation to conduct hypocritical deeds of the flesh to win men's approval. Examine my heart, explore the personal reasons for my thoughts, and uncover all that offends You. Help me live and work for Your honor and glory from now on, in Jesus's name, AMEN.

DAY ONE HUNDRED AND SIXTEEN

ALONGSIDE A MIRACLE-WORKING GOD

You are the God who performs miracles; you display your power among the peoples.
Psalm 77:14

S mith Wigglesworth, the British Evangelist, used to sing a simple song whenever he preached from the Word,

Only believe, only believe, all things are possible, only believe,
Lord I believe, Lord I believe, all things are possible, Lord I believe.

These simple lines contain faith statements coming right from the heart of this preacher. God delights in showing His power to His people. Every act of God is wondrous and can be comprehended only by His own wisdom.

We value the spectacular things God does, but the greatest miracle is when we work alongside a miracle-working God. This miracle happens inside us. We become God's partner in bringing change within us and around us. Being God's channel changes the level of our faith and increases our capacity for divine manifestations.

PRAYER

I thank you, Almighty God, for your promises and praise you for your majesty. I bring all my problems to you; rescue me from them all. May I behold your miracles in my life. I pray in Jesus's name. Amen.

DAY ONE HUNDRED AND SEVENTEEN

A NEW COMMAND, THE MOST IMPORTANT COMMAND

A new command I give you: Love one another. As I have loved you, so you must love one another.
John 13:34

Jesus is introducing a command that we also see in the Old Testament. However, the difference is Jesus is living out that love. He's leading by example.

Jesus escalated the requirement of the law to something which is required for every Jesus follower. It's part of the New Covenant that Jesus ratified with his blood on the cross. Our sacrificial love for others should be the distinguishing factor of our Christianity. We follow a God that gave up his life, not because we deserved it, but because we needed it.

PRAYER

Father, may I live in spirit and truth, and may I surrender to the Holy Spirit and obey Your will, as Christ did. May I love as Christ loves so that I become nothing. May Christ be seen in me and may I put forth His love in my life, to Your honor and glory. AMEN, I pray in Jesus's name.

DAY ONE HUNDRED AND EIGHTEEN

THE SPIRIT HELPS US IN OUR WEAKNESS

In the same way, the Spirit helps us in our weakness. We do not know what we ought to pray for, but the Spirit himself intercedes for us through wordless groans.
Romans 8:26

In the same way, the Spirit helps us in our weakness. We do not know what we ought to pray, but the Spirit himself intercedes for us through wordless groans. We cannot essentially accomplish anything worthwhile in life unless the Holy Spirit works through us, and the key to that is prayer. One of the key roles of the Holy Spirit is to help us pray.

We often fail to comprehend God's will, His plans, and His greater purpose in our lives. The Spirit connects our prayers with those missing and mysterious elements. The Spirit situates the weakness of our prayers within the strength of God's intentions.

PRAYER

Thank You, Father, for Your indwelling Holy Spirit, Who understands my heart better than I know myself. Thank You that He is currently interceding for me with groans that cannot be spoken. Take my inner yearnings and beautify them, I pray, so that I might live my life in a way that honors You. AMEN, in Jesus's name.

DAY ONE HUNDRED AND NINETEEN

A BETTER COVENANT

For this is the covenant that I will make with the house of Israel after those days, says the Lord: I will put My laws in their mind and write them on their hearts, and I will be their God, and they shall be My people.
Hebrews 8:10

God desired a relationship when He created man and established the nation, Israel. God even established a covenant with them. However, the children of Israel failed to keep the covenant. So, it became necessary for God to establish a new covenant, which He brought through His Son, Jesus Christ.

The New Covenant which God gave differed from the previous one. This time, it was a response that came out of their hearts, a desire to please God and to serve God.

God writes His laws on our hearts and then encourages us and empowers us to keep them. His joy is seeing us keep the covenant not as a burden but as a privilege. In the new covenant, God's Spirit within us has written the law in our hearts and causes us to walk in His statutes.

PRAYER

Father, keep us completely dependent upon You for the strength and the desire to obey Your laws. We thank You that the covenant between us is not dependent upon us but upon You. Thank you for the Holy Spirit, which guides me and empowers me to obey you and your laws. We love You, Lord. Amen.

DAY ONE HUNDRED AND TWENTY

THE LORD WHO STRENGTHENS

But the Lord stood with me and strengthened me, so that the message might be preached fully through me and that all the Gentiles might hear.
2 Timothy 4:17

When Paul was standing trial before Nero, he was literally forsaken by his friends. "At my first defense, no one stood with me," he said, "but all forsook me." (2 Timothy 4:16).

The Bible says that "a friend loves at all times" (Proverbs 17:17), but too often, we discover a difference between true friendship and acquaintances. A true friendship goes beyond the level of knowing each other. In such a friendship, the motive will be how to strengthen the other person.

In Jesus alone, we can find such a friendship. He will always build us up, strengthen us and cover us like no one else can ever do.

When the Lord is with us, we can face tomorrow's trials and future uncertainties.

You might feel deserted, standing alone, and facing an unknown future. Someone once said, "I don't know what tomorrow holds, but I know Who holds tomorrow, and I know Who holds my hand." He will stand with you and see you through.

PRAYER

Father, we thank You that we have such wonderful assurance that You will be with us. Hold us up, Lord, when we think we can't take any more. Hold us with Your right hand.

In Jesus's Name, Amen.

DAY ONE HUNDRED AND TWENTY-ONE

PRIDE GOES BEFORE THE FALL

Pride goes before destruction, and a haughty spirit before stumbling
Proverb 16:18

Pride is destructive. Pride says, "I can do it myself. I don't need God to come out of this mess." Pride is a false confidence placed on self. On the contrary, humility is confidence placed in God. A proud person is often all by himself, whereas a humble person enjoys the grace of God, which is essential for success.

Pride in our life is defeated by our dependency on God and others. Delighting in the Lord and humbly following His commands makes us surefooted so we will not slip.

PRAYER

Loving Lord! may nothing separate me from You today. Teach me to choose only Your way today so each step will lead me closer to You. Help me walk by the Word and not my feelings. Help me keep my heart pure and undivided. Let my life be marked by a humble spirit today. Forgive me for my proud, self-centered ways and independent spirit. In Jesus's name I pray, AMEN.

DAY ONE HUNDRED AND TWENTY-TWO

GOD GUIDES THE OUTCOME OF ALL WHAT WE DO

Ship your grain across the sea; after many days you may receive a return.
Ecclesiastes 11:1

We need balance in our lives. Some people concentrate so much on being productive and achieving something they seem to have no enjoyment of life. Others are so consumed with enjoying life they seem to waste opportunities to invest in being productive for God's Kingdom. God has designed our lives to be both productive and enjoyable.

The wisdom of Ecclesiastes suggests two facts. The first is that whatever we do in life, there will be a reward.

The second fact we should be aware of is that it takes some time before we see results for anything we do.

Life is fleeting and fragile. We live and act with trust, enjoying things that can simply be enjoyed now and believing that God, not us, guides the outcomes. We must trust God with what we can't control. God knows how to make it all work out. He is in complete control.

PRAYER

Dear, Lord! Thank you for this day and a chance for a new start. Yesterday is gone, and with it, any regrets, mistakes, or failures. It's a good day to be glad and give thanks, and I do, Lord. Thank you for today, a new opportunity to love, give, and be all you want me to be. Lord our God, help us trust you in all circumstances. We know you have absolute control over every small and big thing pertaining to me and what I do. Help me trust that you work everything for good. In Jesus's name! Amen.

DAY ONE HUNDRED AND TWENTY-THREE

THE MOUTH SPEAKS WHAT THE HEART IS FULL OF …

To show partiality is not good, yet a person will do wrong for a piece of bread.
Proverbs 28:21

The book of Psalms guides us on how we can talk to God. Each of these Psalms are from personal experience. On the other hand, the book of Proverbs was given so that we have a valued inter-personal relationship. They tell us how to speak to each other. Most of the proverbs reveal how delicate and complex human relationships are.

It's often a challenge to know what to say to each other, and sometimes we get it wrong: saying the wrong things for the wrong reasons and even saying right things for the wrong reasons.

We shouldn't be playing favorites, and it's also not good to act with false motives. To say what someone else wants to hear just to keep the peace or to gain a reward—even for a small thing like a bread—can be deceitful and corrupt.

Jesus teaches that "the mouth speaks what the heart is full of" (Luke 6:45). If we are satisfied by the bread of life that only Jesus can give, we will speak truth.

PRAYER

Heavenly Father, thank you for your amazing power and work in our lives. Thank you for your goodness and for your blessings over us. Thank you for your great love and care. Thank you for your sacrifice so that we might have freedom and life. Forgive us when we don't thank you enough, for who you are, for all you do, and for all you've given. Help us set our eyes and our hearts on you afresh. Renew our spirits and fill us with your peace and joy. Help us speak truth and help us resist speaking falsely or doing wrong just to please others. In Jesus's Name, Amen.

9 7 9 8 9 8 7 7 3 0 3 0 0